U.S. Mint

# Miscellaneous Letters Received from 1897 to 1903

Vol. 12

U.S. Mint

**Miscellaneous Letters Received from 1897 to 1903**
*Vol. 12*

ISBN/EAN: 9783337817138

Printed in Europe, USA, Canada, Australia, Japan

Cover: Foto ©Suzi / pixelio.de

More available books at **www.hansebooks.com**

# RG 104, 8KRA-104-84-042
# Box 6, Volume XII

Miscellaneous Letters Received,
1897-1903. Letters Received Relating
to the Construction of the New Denver
Mint, 1897-1906.

Form No. 168.

# THE WESTERN UNION TELEGRAPH COMPANY.

INCORPORATED

23,000 OFFICES IN AMERICA. CABLE SERVICE TO ALL THE WORLD.

This Company TRANSMITS and DELIVERS messages only on conditions limiting its liability, which have been assented to by the sender of the following message. Errors can be guarded against only by repeating a message back to the sending station for comparison, and the Company will not hold itself liable for errors or delays in transmission or delivery of Unrepeated Messages, beyond the amount of tolls paid thereon, nor in any case where the claim is not presented in writing within sixty days after the message is filed with the Company for transmission.
This is an UNREPEATED MESSAGE, and is delivered by request of the sender, under the conditions named above.
ROBERT C. CLOWRY, President and General Manager.

**RECEIVED** at 1114 to 1118 17th St., Denver, Colo.
TELEPHONES MAIN 4444, 4445 AND 4446.

19 a.jw.m. 23 paid Govt

Washington DC dec 19-1904

Custodian New Mint, Denver, Col.

Wire when all unfinished items faith contract per telegram December seventeenth are completed

J.K.Taylor, Supervising Architect.

322pm

Form No. 168.

# THE WESTERN UNION TELEGRAPH COMPANY.

INCORPORATED

23,000 OFFICES IN AMERICA. CABLE SERVICE TO ALL THE WORLD.

This Company TRANSMITS and DELIVERS messages only on conditions limiting its liability, which have been assented to by the sender of the following message. Errors can be guarded against only by repeating a message back to the sending station for comparison, and the Company will not hold itself liable for errors or delays in transmission or delivery of Unrepeated Messages, beyond the amount of tolls paid thereon, nor in any case where the claim is not presented in writing within sixty days after the message is filed with the Company for transmission.
This is an UNREPEATED MESSAGE, and is delivered by request of the sender, under the conditions named above.
ROBERT C. CLOWRY, President and General Manager.

**RECEIVED** at 1114 to 1118 17th St., Denver, Colo.
TELEPHONES MAIN 4444, 4445 AND 4446.

1017-CH.KQ.MZ. 40 PAID GOVT.

K.WASHINGTON.D.C.DEC. 17th

Custodian NewMint Denver Colo.

Items seven nine twenty one thirty four fifty one fifty five sixty seventy office letter november seventeenth adjusted by office wire if all others items said letter are satisfactorily complete

1155a- J.K.TAYLOR. Supervising Architect

ALWAYS OPEN. MONEY TRANSFERRED BY TELEGRAPH. CABLE OFFICE

THE WESTERN UNION TELEGRAPH COMPANY.

INCORPORATED

23,000 OFFICES IN AMERICA. CABLE SERVICE TO ALL THE WORLD.

[illegible]

ROBERT C. CLOWRY, President and General Manager.

RECEIVED at 1114 to 1118 17th St., Denver, Colo.

TELEPHONES MAIN [illegible]

[illegible] 47 Paid Govt.

[illegible]

Custodian, New Mint, Denver, Colo.

Notify Faith & Co. that item 65 is waived,
but require them to complete item 38 at once
It not being deemed necessary to postpone this work
until engine room floor is laid. Wire results.

J.K.Taylor, Supervising Architect.

340 p.m.

THE WESTERN UNION TELEGRAPH COMPANY.

INCORPORATED

23,000 OFFICES IN AMERICA. CABLE SERVICE TO ALL THE WORLD.

[illegible]

ROBERT C. CLOWRY, President and General Manager.

RECEIVED at 1114 to 1118 17th St., Denver, Colo.

TELEPHONES MAIN [illegible]

[illegible] 10 pd

Leavenworth, Kas., Jany 12-05

[illegible] Cowmen, Custodian, [illegible] Bldg., Denver

When did you forward my vouchers mint building to Washington.

James [illegible] McGonigle

12:44PM

[illegible] MONEY TRANSFERRED BY TELEGRAPH. CABLE OFFICE.

Office of Superintendent of ............

U.S. ............

SUBJECT

# McPhee & McGinnity Co.,

ESTABLISHED 1872. INCORPORATED 1904

LUMBER

OFFICE & FACTORY 18TH & WAZEE STREETS.

Denver, Colo. Dec. 27, 1904.

Custodian U.S. Mint Bldg.,

Denver, Colo.

Dear Sir:-

We are in receipt of a letter from the Van Kannel Revolving Door Co. who state that they furnish the doors to the Government at the same price they would furnish them to us. As this is a class of work which is entirely out of our line, we will, therefore, be unable to make you as good a figure as you can get direct from them. We wish, however, to thank you for giving us an opportunity to figure on this.

Yours truly,
McPhee & McGinnity Co.,
By [signature] Secy.

WHR

F. M. DILLON. W. G. WILSON.

# THE DILLON IRON WORKS Co

**Steam and Water Power Plants.**

## MINING, MILLING AND GENERAL MACHINERY

'PHONE 1621. 1825-27-29-31 BLAKE ST.

CRUSHERS. STAMP MILLS.
ROLLS. SCREENS.
CONCENTRATORS.
HOISTS.
&C.

DENVER, COLO.,

December 27th 1904

Custodian

New U. S. Mint

City

QUOTATION.

We have pleasure in quoting you as follows on Iron Grills for Mint Bldg.

Grills as per design A, hinged, and fitted with Yale Lock, supplied and fitted in place for the sum of $44.10 each (Fortyfour dollars and ten cents each)

Grills as per design B anchored in place with four bolts as shown for the sum of $34.20 each (Thirtyfour dollars and twenty cents each) supplied and fitted in place.

Grills to be supplied and fitted in place as per blueprints herewith.

Yours truly

The Dillon Iron Works Co

per [signature]

WGW-W

DENVER NEW MINT.

OFFICE OF SUPERVISING ARCHITECT

IN REPLYING, QUOTE UPPER INITIAL, RIGHT HAND CORNER.

TREASURY DEPARTMENT

WASHINGTON January 5, 1905.

Enclosure 2595.

The Custodian,
U. S. Mint (New),
Denver, Colorado.

Sir:

Referring to your telegram of the 3rd instant, and to office wire of the same day, relative to the completion of items 38 and 65, in the defects and omissions under the contract with S. Faith and Company, for the mechanical equipment at the building in your custody, enclosed find copy of a letter this day addressed to the contractors, in amplification, the purport of which is self-explanatory.

You are requested to advise the office when item 38 has been completed.

Respectfully,

Supervising Architect.

DENVER NEW MINT.
V.

OFFICE OF SUPERVISING ARCHITECT

IN REPLYING, QUOTE UPPER INITIAL, RIGHT HAND CORNER.

S.

TREASURY DEPARTMENT

WASHINGTON January 5,1905.

Messrs. S. Faith and Company,
2427 Pennsylvania Avenue,
Philadelphia, Pennsylvania.

Sirs:

Referring to communication addressed to you on November 17th last, itemizing the defects and omissions found to exist in your contract for the mechanical equipment, at the New Mint, Denver, Colorado, you are advised that the Custodian of the building, by wire, dated the 3rd instant, states that all items have been corrected and supplied, except No.38, the setting up and connecting of the gauge board for engine room and the gauges and clock for same, and No.65, the test with back gear drive and maximum load of elevator No.1, after the engine and generators are in service in the building.

In regard to the first item, you are advised that the office recedes from the position taken which required the completion of the work, after the engine room floor is laid, and you are now directed to install the gauge board, &c., immediately, as it has been deemed unnecessary to postpone this work until the floor is laid.

Referring to the second item, No.66, you are advised that as all tests of elevator No.1, with back gears in and out were made, except the maximum load test with back gears in, the latter test will be waived, as it is believed that the test with maximum load, with back gears out, is substantially the same as that test with back gears in. It is also understood that the latter test could not be made prior to March 1sy next, as the main engines and generators will probably not be in commission before that time, and the office does not desire to work a hardship upon you by deferring final settlement pending the test indicated.

A copy of this letter will be forwarded to the Custodian of the building, and its purport was telegraphed to him on yesterday, and when he advises the office that item No.38, has received your attention, consideration will be given to final settlement.

Respectfully,

(Signed) J. K. Taylor

Supervising Architect.

C. E. R.

L.

DENVER, NEW MINT

Q.

IN REPLYING, QUOTE UPPER INITIAL RIGHT HAND CORNER.

Inclosure No. 3089

TREASURY DEPARTMENT

WASHINGTON, Jan. 9, 1905.

Custodian,

U. S. Mint (New),

Denver, Colorado.

Sir:

Referring further to the completion of work under the contract with S. Faith & Company for the mechanical equipment at the building in your custody, inclosed find copy of a communication this day addressed to them in relation to the installation of the guage board and the guarantee of elevator No. 1, which will explain itself.

As soon as the guage board indicated has been installed satisfactorily in place, you are requested to advise the Office to that effect in order that consideration may be given to final settlement.

Respectfully,

Supervising Architect.

DENVER, NEW MINT

OFFICE OF SUPERVISING ARCHITECT

IN REPLYING QUOTE UPPER INITIAL, RIGHT HAND CORNER.

TREASURY DEPARTMENT

WASHINGTON , Jan. 9, 1905.

Messrs. S. Faith & Co.,

2427 Pennsylvania Avenue,

Philadelphia, Pennsylvania.

Sirs:

Your communication of the 6th instant is hereby acknowledged, in which you advise the Office that you have wired your representative to at once set and connect gauge board in engine room, under the terms of your contract for the mechanical equipment for the new Mint at Denver, Colorado; also, that you guarantee the operation of elevator No. 1, under maximum load with back gears in, for a period of six months from the 6th instant, and that during said period you will, without expense to the Government, correct any defects (except those incident to ordinary wear and tear) in the operation of the elevator with back gears in service.

The guarantee indicated is satisfactory to the Office, and, as soon as the Custodian of the building reports the completion of the gauge board, consideration will then be given to final settlement under the terms of your contract.

A copy of this letter has been transmitted to the Custodian of the building for his information.

Respectfully,

Denver, Colo., Jan. 19, 1905.

Custodian,

U.S. Mint.

Sir:-

I hereby propose to repair plastering in engine room ceiling where damaged by traveling crane and make same satisfactory, for the sum of Twelve Dollars.

(Signed) J.B. Lanyon,

Plasterer, 3720 Milwaukee Street,

Denver, Colorado.

John H. Selmes,
Prest & Treas'r.

ESTABLISHED 1854.

George B. Coggeshall

# The Mitchell Vance Company,

Manufacturers and Importers of

## Lighting Fixtures for Electricity & Gas

THE
ARCHER AND PANCOAST COMPANY
ASSOCIATED.

836 & 838, Broadway

ADDRESS CORRESPONDENCE
MANUFACTORY
10TH AVE. 24TH & 25TH STS.

New York, Jan. 28/1905

U. S. Mint,

Denver, Colo.

Gentlemen;

We are in receipt of your letter of Jan.25th. stating that there are switches in our fixtures put up by sub-contractors that do not work and you have called their attention to the fact several times and they have not fixed them.

We regret to learn this and will to-day communicate with them at once, and request them to take steps at once to put this work in a satisfactory condition, as we should like very much to have a final settlement of the bill.

Yours truly,

The Mitchell Vance Company,

Sec'y.

DENVER, NEW MINT.

OFFICE OF SUPERVISING ARCHITECT

IN REPLYING QUOTE UPPER INITIAL, RIGHT HAND CORNER

TREASURY DEPARTMENT

WASHINGTON Jan. 28, 1905.

Custodian,
New Mint Building,
Denver, Colorado.

Sir:-

In view of the approval of this Department, you are hereby authorized to accept the proposal of Mr. J. B. Lanyon, inclosed in your letter of the 19th instant, in amount twelve dollars ($12.00), for making good the damage to plaster on ceiling in engine room in the building in your custody, a public exigency requiring the immediate performance of the work; and you are hereby authorized to certify and issue vouchers for the work, after its satisfactory completion by the contractor, in the usual manner, and forward the same to this Department for payment charged against the appropriation for Mint Building, Denver, Colorado.

Respectfully,

Acting Supervising Architect.

KCH

DENVER MINT (NEW)

IN REPLYING, QUOTE UPPER INITIAL, RIGHT HAND CORNER.

TREASURY DEPARTMENT

Inclosure 3963. WASHINGTON January 18, 1905.

Custodian,
Mint Building (New),
Denver, Colorado.

Sir:-

I have to inform you that the Department, on the 17th instant, waived the provision in contract dated August 9, 1902, with Messrs. S. Faith and Company, stipulating the per diem amount of liquidated damages for delay in completion of the mechanical equipment for the building in your custody, and authorized the payment of $26,402.90, the balance outstanding under the contract, and proposals accepted in addition thereto.

There is inclosed, therefore, to be certified by you, and receipted by the contractors and returned to the Department, two (2) vouchers, duly prepared, aggregating the amount stated above, one for $18,260.50, payable from the appropriation for "Mint Building, Denver, Colorado," and the other for $8,142.40, payable from the appropriation for "New Machinery, Denver Mint."

Respectfully,

Chief Executive Officer.

G.

THE MOUNTAIN ELECTRIC COMPANY,

Denver,Colo.,January 31,1905.

Custodian of the Mint,

Denver, Colorado.

Dear Sir:-

We will furnish and mount upon the switchboard in the Denver Mint two 3 point ground detector switches for use in connection with your present voltmeter ground detectors, these switches to be mounted upon the back and operated from the front; all front work to be copper plated and the construction to be similar to the voltmeter switches already in use upon the board.

Price mounted complete and connected, Sixteen Dollars ($16.00).

Hoping to receive your order,

Yours very truly,

The Mountain Electric Company,

E.A.Rainous.

DENVER NEW MINT.

THE SUPERVISING ARCHITECT

IN REPLYING, QUOTE UPPER INITIAL, RIGHT HAND CORNER.

TREASURY DEPARTMENT

OFFICE OF THE SECRETARY

WASHINGTON Feb.6,1905.

Disbursing Agent,
New Mint Building,
Denver,Colorado.

Sir:

The Department has this day accepted the proposal of The Dillon Iron Works Co.of your City,the lower of two received, in amount one hundred and twelve dollars and fifty cents ($112.50), to furnish and place iron grilles over the large area windows on the east side of the building, a public exigency requiring the immediate performance of the work;and you are hereby authorized to make payment therefor,upon vouchers properly certified and issued by the Custodian, in the usual manner, from funds remitted you on account of the appropriation for Mint Building,Denver,Colorado.

Respectfully,

H. A. Taylor

Assistant Secretary.

T.
J.C.P.

JSS

DENVER, NEW MINT

OFFICE OF SUPERVISING ARCHITECT

IN REPLYING, QUOTE UPPER INITIAL, RIGHT HAND CORNER.

TREASURY DEPARTMENT

WASHINGTON Feb.9,1905.

Custodian,
New Mint Building,
Denver, Colorado.

Sir:

I have to acknowledge receipt of your letter of the 14th ultimo forwarding a proposal, in amount $765.00 for doors at main entrance of the building in your custody, and you are requested to reject the proposal, inasmuch as the balance of the appropriation is inadequate to meet the expense.

Respectfully,

Supervising Architect.

HM

DENVER NEW MINT

OFFICE OF SUPERVISING ARCHITECT

FORWARDING

IN REPLYING, QUOTE UPPER INITIAL, RIGHT HAND CORNER.

TREASURY DEPARTMENT

WASHINGTON Feb. 8, 1905.

Custodian,
New Mint Building,
Denver, Colorado.

Sir:

There are forwarded herewith, under separate cover, six copies of drawing #290 and specifications for reinforcement of first floor vault in Weigh Clerk's room of the building in your custody, and you are requested to obtain competitive proposals based thereon and forward them to this Office with your definite recommendation.

Respectfully,

J K Taylor
Supervising Architect.

HM

d twelve dollars and fifty cents $[illegible]
the [illegible] iron grilles over the large [illegible]
st side of the building in your custody, [illegible]
you are hereby authorized to certify an
for the work, after its satisfactory comp
the usual manner, payment of which voucher
gent has been authorized to make from the
[illegible] Building, Denver, Col. [illegible] Please [illegible]
this action

Respectfully,

[illegible]

Feb. 8, 1905.

The Dillon Iron Works Co.,
1825 Blake Street,
Denver, Colorado.

Gentlemen:

In view of the statement and recommendation contained in letter of the 18th ultimo, from the Custodian of the new Mint Building at Denver, Colorado, and in accordance with the approval of this Department, your proposal, dated December 27, 1904, the lower of two received under circular letter, is hereby accepted to furnish and place iron grilles over the large area windows on the east side of the building, two to be fixed and one hinged, respectively, as may be directed by the custodian, for the total sum of one hundred and twelve dollars and fifty cents ($112.50), a public exigency requiring the immediate performance of the work, which will be paid for after its completion by you and acceptance by the Government from the appropriation for Mint Building, Denver, Colorado.

Please acknowledge the receipt of this letter, a copy of which will be forwarded to the Custodian.

Respectfully,

DENVER, NEW MINT

Q

OFFICE OF SUPERVISING ARCHITECT

IN REPLYING, QUOTE UPPER INITIAL RIGHT HAND CORNER.

Inclosure No. 3638

TREASURY DEPARTMENT

S

WASHINGTON, Feb. 15, 1905.

The Custodian,

New Mint,

Denver, Colorado.

Sir:

Inclosed find copy of a communication this day addressed to Mr. James A. McGonigle, Contractor for the interior finish, etc., of the building in your custody, making demand upon him to properly drain the floor of the cellar for sweeps, etc., at the building, and you are requested to advise the Office on the 15th proximo if the necessary remedies have been applied, and if not, the Government will then proceed to correct the conditions at the Contractor's expense.

You are also requested, when the Contractor commences to correct the conditions, to have some one at the building competent to pass upon the work supervise the same, in order that the floor may be properly drained to the dry wells.

Respectfully,

Supervising Architect.

DENVER, NEW MINT

THE SUPERVISING ARCHITECT

IN REPLYING, QUOTE UPPER INITIAL, RIGHT HAND CORNER.

TREASURY DEPARTMENT

OFFICE OF THE SECRETARY

WASHINGTON, Feb. 1[illegible], 1906.

Mr. James A. McGonigle,

Leavenworth,

Kansas.

Sir:

Referring to the recent action of the Department in requesting a certified check from you, in the sum of $500.00, before making final settlement under the terms of your contract for the interior finish, etc., of the new Mint at Denver, Colorado, you are advised that the proceeds of said check have been deposited with the Treasurer of the United States, and will be held subject to your carrying out the provisions of the terms of your contract relative to the storage cellar for the sweeps, etc., your proposal for which was accepted on March 12, 1904, as an addition to your original contract.

From reports received from the Mint officials, and from a representative of the Department who recently made an examination of the conditions, it is learned that the object for which the sweeps cellar is intended is defeated to some extent by reason of the fact that the floor does not properly drain to the two dry wells, it being reported that water stands in spots near the walls and in other places.

The tenor of drawing No. 247-A contemplates the proper drainage of the floor to the dry wells, and it is also of record that the Superintendent of Construction in charge of the work, recognizing the fact that the floor should be so drained, directed your representative to properly drain the floor to the dry wells, and the very fact that dry wells were required should have suggested to you the necessity for properly draining the floor to same, to secure the object for which the sweeps cellar was installed.

For the above reason, therefore, the Department deems that you are responsible for the correction of the present condition, and as you have indicated a willingness, in your letter of the 11th instant, to apply the necessary remedy, when the weather moderates, the date when the work must be completed is fixed at not later than March 15th, next.

A copy of this letter has been transmitted to the Custodian of the building, and when he reports the satisfactory correction of the floor, and its proper drainage to the dry wells, the proceeds of the certified check deposited by you will be returned. If, however, you fail to respond favorably to this demand on or before the 15th proximo, the work will be done by the Government from the proceeds of the check deposited, and the balance, should there be any, returned to you.

Respectfully,

(Signed) H. A. Taylor,

Assistant Secretary.

DENVER, COLO., NEW MINT.

OFFICE OF SUPERVISING ARCHITECT

IN REPLYING QUOTE UPPER INITIAL, RIGHT HAND CORNER

TREASURY DEPARTMENT

WASHINGTON Feb. 18, 1905.

Custodian,
New Mint Building,
Denver, Colo.

Sir:-

In view of the approval of this Department and the recommendation contained in your letter of the 9th instant, you are hereby authorized to accept the proposal of the Mountain Electric Company, to furnish and mount upon switch board, two 3-point ground detector switches, for use in connection with voltmeter ground detectors now in the building in your custody, as fully set forth in their proposal, for the sum of sixteen dollars ($16.00), a public exigency requiring the same; and you are hereby authorized to certify and issue vouchers therefor, in accordance with the printed "Instructions to Custodians", payment of which the Disbursing Agent has been authorized to make from the appropriation for New Mint, Denver, Colorado.

Respectfully,

Supervising Architect.

DENVER, NEW MINT.

THE SUPERVISING ARCHITECT

IN REPLYING QUOTE UPPER INITIAL RIGHT HAND CORNER

# TREASURY DEPARTMENT

OFFICE OF THE SECRETARY

WASHINGTON Feb. 18, 1905.

Disbursing Agent,
New Mint Building,
Denver, Colo.

Sir:-

The Department has this day authorized the Custodian of the New Mint building in your city, to accept the proposal of the Mountain Electric Company, to furnish and mount upon switch board, two 3-point ground detector switches at the New Mint building in your city, for the sum of sixteen dollars ($16.00), a public exigency requiring the same; and you are hereby authorized to make payment therefor, on vouchers properly issued and certified by the Custodian, in the usual manner, from funds remitted you on account of the appropriation for New Mint, Denver, Colorado.

Respectfully,

Assistant Secretary.

Paid
March 25 1905

T.
J.C.P.
KCH

DENVER, MINT (NEW).

OFFICE OF SUPERVISING ARCHITECT

IN REPLYING, QUOTE UPPER INITIAL, RIGHT HAND CORNER.

TREASURY DEPARTMENT

WASHINGTON March 9, 1905.

Custodian,
U. S. Mint,
Denver, Colo.

Sir:-

The Secretary of the Treasury, on the 8th instant, having waived the provision in contract dated May 14, 1904, with The Mitchell Vance Company, stipulating the per diem amount of liquidated damages for delay in furnishing and placing, complete, the lighting fixtures for the building in your custody, you are hereby directed to prepare, certify, and issue a voucher in favor of the company for $1,449.50, the balance outstanding under the contract, and, when duly receipted, to forward it to the Department for payment, charged against the appropriation for "New Machinery, Denver Mint."

The following is a statement of the account:-

| | | |
|---|---|---|
| Contract dated May 14, 1904. | For lighting fixtures, | $7,247.50 |
| Less payments on account,........................................ | | 5,798.00 |
| Balance due,..................................................... | | $1,449.50 |

Respectfully,

[signature]

Chief Executive Officer.

G.

IN REPLYING, QUOTE UPPER INITIAL, RIGHT HAND CORNER.

# TREASURY DEPARTMENT

L-o-s

WASHINGTON March 10,1905.

19

FORWARDING.
J.B.S.

The Custodian,

U. S. Mint Building,

Denver, Colorado.

Sir:

In accordance with the request contained in your letter of the 1st instant, there has this day been forwarded for your information and files a print of drawing No.286, showing the floor framing for the engine room in the building under your custody.

Respectfully,

J K Taylor
Supervising Architect.

M.

L
Clerk

DENVER NEW MINT.

OFFICE OF SUPERVISING ARCHITECT

IN REPLYING, QUOTE UPPER INITIAL, RIGHT HAND CORNER.

TREASURY DEPARTMENT

WASHINGTON March 16, 1905.

Inclosure No. 1249.

Custodian,
New Mint Building,
Denver, Colo.

Sir:-

There is inclosed herewith, for your information and the files of your office, copy of Department letter of even date, accepting the proposal of Mr. James Cramer, in amount one hundred and seventy-five dollars ($175.00), the lowest of six received under circular letter, to furnish all the labor and materials required to reinforce first floor vault in the building in your custody, in strict accordance with drawing #290, such work to be completed by May 31, 1905; and you are hereby authorized to certify and issue vouchers therefor, after the satisfactory completion of the work and its acceptance by the Government, in accordance with the printed "Instructions to Custodians", and forward such vouchers to this Department for payment, charged against the appropriation for Mint Building, Denver, Colorado.

Please advise the other bidders of this action.

Respectfully,

Mr. James Cramer,
#3435 Stout Street,
Denver, Colorado.

Sir:

In view of the statement and recommendation contained in letter of the 27th ultimo, from the Custodian of the New Mint Building at Denver, Colorado, and in accordance with the approval of this Department, your proposal, dated the 25th ultimo, the lowest of six received under circular letter, in amount one hundred and seventy-five dollars ($175.00), is hereby accepted to furnish all the labor and materials required to reinforce first floor vault in the said building, in strict accordance with drawing #290, the specification, and the instructions of the Custodian, a public exigency requiring the immediate performance of the work, which it is understood and agreed is to be completed by May 31, 190[illegible], and paid for, after its satisfactory completion by you and acceptance by the Government, from the appropriation for Mint Building, Denver, Colorado.

Please acknowledge the receipt of this letter, a copy of which will be forwarded to the Custodian.

Respectfully,

Assistant Secretary.

T.
J. [illegible] P.

JSS

POSTAL TELEGRAPH — COMMERCIAL CABLES

CLARENCE H. MACKAY, PRESIDENT.

# TELEGRAM

350

REGISTERED TRADE-MARK. DESIGN PATENT, NO. 36369.

The Postal Telegraph-Cable Company (Incorporated) transmits and delivers this message subject to the terms and conditions printed on the back of this blank.

*Received at Main Office, 920 17th Street, Ernest & Cranmer Building, Denver.* (TELEPHONES 4600, 4601).

[illegible] 23 Govt---[illegible]a

Washington D. C. Mar 21-0[illegible]

Custodian New Mint

Denver Colo.

McGonigle wires that he has telegraphed to Denver to correct sweep room cellar advise offices.

J. K. Taylor

Sup Architect

---

POSTAL TELEGRAPH — COMMERCIAL CABLES

CLARENCE H. MACKAY, PRESIDENT.

# TELEGRAM

#66 467

REGISTERED TRADE-MARK. DESIGN PATENT, NO. 36369.

The Postal Telegraph-Cable Company (Incorporated) transmits and delivers this message subject to the terms and conditions printed on the back of this blank.

*Received at Main Office, 920 17th Street, Ernest & Cranmer Building, Denver.* (TELEPHONES 4600, 4601).

[illegible] Govt [illegible]p

W[illegible] DC Mar [illegible]

Supt New Mint;

Denver Colo

C[illegible] McGonigle [illegible] sweep cellar floor [illegible]

[illegible]

J K [illegible], Sup[illegible] Arch[illegible]

DENVER MINT (NEW)

MGD

TREASURY DEPARTMENT

IN REPLYING, QUOTE UPPER INITIAL, RIGHT HAND CORNER.

WASHINGTON March 21, 1905.

The Custodian,

U. S. Mint (New),

Denver, Col.

Sir:

Through error of the mailing room, this office, a set of plans and specifications for the mechanical equipment of the building in your custody, intended for transmission to Baltimore, Md., was sent to Batesville, Ark., and thence to the Denver Mint, addressed to the Superintendent of Construction. As another set has been supplied for the purpose for which this set was intended, you need not return the set to this office, but may leave it on file at the building.

Respectfully,

Supervising Architect.

DENVER NEW MINT.

OFFICE OF SUPERVISING ARCHITECT

IN REPLYING, QUOTE UPPER INITIAL RIGHT HAND CORNER.

B

Inclosure 2320

TREASURY DEPARTMENT

WASHINGTON Mar.30,1905.

Custodian,
New Mint Building,
Denver,Colorado.

Sir:

I inclose herewith, for your information and the files of your office, a copy of a letter of even date, accepting the proposal of the Diebold Safe & Lock Co.,in amount eighty-nine dollars and twenty-five cents ($89.25), as an addition to their contract for new door for vault in Weigh Clerk's room in the building in your custody, for changes in vestibule,etc.,as recommended by your endorsement,dated March 17,1905,on their said proposal;and you are hereby authorized to certify and issue vouchers for the work,as required by the terms of the contract,in the usual manner,and to forward them to this Department for payment,charged against the appropriation for Mint Building,Denver,Colorado.

In this connection you are requested to obtain a proposal to have the floor of the vault made level with the floor of the vestibule,and forward same to this Office at once with your recommendation.

Respectfully,

Supervising Architect.

JSS

Diebold Safe and Lock Co.,
Canton, Ohio.

Gentlemen:

In accordance with the recommendation of the Superintendent of the Mint, Denver, Colorado, your proposal, dated March 6, 1905, addressed to the Supervising Architect, in amount eighty-nine dollars and twenty-five cents ($89.25), is hereby accepted, as an addition to your contract for new door for vault in the Weigh Clerk's room in the new Mint Building in the said City, for changes in vestibule, etc., in accordance with the terms of your proposal, a public exigency requiring the immediate performance of the work.

It is understood and agreed that this acceptance is not to affect the time for the completion of the work as required by the terms of your contract; that the same is without prejudice to any and all rights of the United States thereunder; and without prejudice, also, to any and all rights of the United States against the sureties on the bond executed for the faithful fulfillment of the contract.

Please acknowledge the receipt of this letter, a copy of which will be forwarded to the Custodian.

Respectfully,

Assistant Secretary.

T.
J.C.P.

JSS

DENVER, NEW MINT

OFFICE OF SUPERVISING ARCHITECT

IN REPLYING, QUOTE UPPER INITIAL, RIGHT HAND CORNER

TREASURY DEPARTMENT

WASHINGTON April 1,1905.

Custodian,
New Mint,
Denver, Colorado.

Sir:

I have to acknowledge your letter of the 20th ultimo relative to leaking of storm water through coal hole covers at the building in your custody, and you are requested to obtain proposals for the scheme which in your opinion will remedy the trouble, and forward them to this Office with your definite recommendation, together with a full description of the method it is proposed to follow.

As the balance of the appropriation is extremely limited it is not known whether there will be funds to cover the expense of said work, but full consideration will be given to the matter upon receipt of the information requested.

Respectfully,

Supervising Architect.

HM

(Ed. 1-18-1904—250,000.)

No. 1765. TREASURY DEPARTMENT

Denver, Colo.,
April 5. 1905.

Supervising Architect,
Treasury Department, Wash. D.C.

I will make the new cement floor in the vault in the Weigh Clerk's room in the U. S. Mint Denver, Colo., new floor to be made level with the floor of ~~said~~ vestibule of said vault for the sum of twenty-five dollars ($25.00)

(Signed Joseph A Seubert
129 W 4 ave
Denver Colo

DENVER, NEW MINT
Q

OFFICE OF SUPERVISING ARCHITECT

IN REPLYING, QUOTE UPPER INITIAL, RIGHT HAND CORNER.

TREASURY DEPARTMENT

S

WASHINGTON, April 8, 1905.

The Custodian,

New Mint,

Denver, Colorado.

Sir:

Referring to your communication of the 4th instant, in relation to correcting the defects in cement floors of the first story, and the wood floor in the Adjusters' room, second story, in the building in your custody, you are advised that Mr. A. A. Packard, Inspector of Public Buildings, will be in Denver about the 17th instant for the purpose of giving these matters his consideration.

Respectfully,

Supervising Architect.

DENVER NEW MINT
M

Inclosure 5667.

TREASURY DEPARTMENT

S

WASHINGTON April 12, 1905.

IN REPLYING, QUOTE UPPER INITIAL, RIGHT HAND CORNER

Custodian,
U. S. Mint (New),
Denver, Colo.

Sir:

There are inclosed herewith copies of Department letters ordering safes for the building in your custody, as follows:

April 11, 1905, to the Hall's Safe Co., for a shell safe with burglar proof chest for the office of the Assayer----------$388.00.

April 12, 1905, to the Macneale & Urban Co., for a shell safe with burglar proof chest for the assay weigh room---------$1081.00.

There are also inclosed copies of the invitations for proposals, dated the 24th ultimo.

These safes were ordered in response to a request from the Director of the Mint, dated the 20th ultimo. Should delivery not be made within the time specified, please call the attention of this office thereto. When each safe is delivered, advise the office to that effect, stating whether in your judgment it is in accordance with the agreement, and if it is, issue a voucher for the expense and forward it here for payment from the appropriation for "Vaults, Safes & Locks for Public Buildings, 1905."

Respectfully,

Supervising Architect.

D[illegible] New Mint
M

THE SUPERVISING ARCHITECT

IN REPLYING, QUOTE UPPER INITIAL, RIGHT HAND CORNER

TREASURY DEPARTMENT

OFFICE OF THE SECRETARY

WASHINGTON April 11, 1905.

The Hall's Safe Co.,
P. O. Box 846,
Cincinnati, Ohio.

Gentlemen:

In accordance with the approval of the Department, your proposal of the 5th instant is hereby accepted in the sum of three hundred and eighty-eight dollars ($388.00) to furnish a shell safe with burglar proof chest and deliver the same in the office of the Assayer in the new U. S. Mint building at Denver, Colo., as provided for by specification No. V and the invitation for bids dated the 24th ultimo; said bid being the lowest of four received and the public exigency requiring the immediate delivery of the article.

The time for delivery is that stated in your proposal, viz., 90 days and is to operate from the 15th instant.

The following locks are to be used: Hall's Monitor sideshaft on the chest, and Hall's 4-tumbler Monitor on the shell safe.

Submit your bill to the Custodian of the building named who will be furnished with a copy of this letter and authorised, upon satisfactory delivery of the safe to issue a voucher for the expense payment of which will be made from the appropriation for "Vaults, Safes & Locks for Public Buildings, 1905."

Respectfully,

(Sgd) H. A. TAYLOR

Assistant Secretary.

DENVER U.S. MINT
M

THE SUPERVISING ARCHITECT

IN REPLYING, QUOTE UPPER INITIAL, RIGHT HAND CORNER

TREASURY DEPARTMENT

OFFICE OF THE SECRETARY

WASHINGTON April 12, 1905.

The Mosler & Urban Co.,
Hamilton, Ohio.

Gentlemen:

In accordance with the approval of the Department, your proposal of the 4th instant is hereby accepted in the sum of ten hundred and eighty-one dollars ($1081.00) to furnish a shell safe with burglar proof chest and deliver the same in the assay weigh room in the new U. S. Mint building at Denver, Colo., as provided for by specification No. V and the invitation dated the 24th ultimo; said bid being the lowest of four received and the public exigency requiring the immediate delivery of the article.

Mosler & Urban No.3, Perfection, bronze case locks are to be used on the chest and shell safe.

This safe is to be delivered on or before June 24, 1905, as stated in the invitation and your proposal, and you are urged to push the work so as to insure delivery by that date.

Submit your bill to the Custodian of the building named, who will be furnished with a copy of this letter and authorized, upon satisfactory delivery of the safe to issue a voucher for the expense, payment of which will be made from the appropriation for "Vaults, Safes & Locks for Public Buildings,1905."

Respectfully,

(Signed) H. A. Taylor

Assistant Secretary.

DENVER,NEW MINT

Inclosure 5645

TREASURY DEPARTMENT

IN REPLYING QUOTE UPPER INITIAL, RIGHT HAND CORNER.

WASHINGTON April 18,1905.

Custodian,
New Mint Building,
Denver, Colorado.

Sir:

There is inclosed herewith, for your information, a copy of letter of even date accepting the proposal of Mr. Joseph A. Seubert, in amount $25.00, to change level of vault floor in Weigh Clerk's room in the building under your custody, as set forth in said letter of acceptance.

You are hereby authorized to certify and issue vouchers on account of the work, after its satisfactory completion and acceptance by the Government, in the usual manner, and to forward them to this Department for payment from the appropriation for Mint Building, Denver, Colorado.

Respectfully,

Supervising Architect.

4
HM

April 18,1905.

Mr. Joseph A. Seubert,
#139 W. 4th Avenue,
Denver, Colorado.

Sir:

In accordance with the approval of this Department your proposal, dated April 5,1905, addressed to the Supervising Architect, in amount twenty-five dollars ($25.00) is hereby accepted to change level of floor in vault in Weigh Clerk's room in the Mint building, Denver, Colorado, to a level with the floor of vestibule of said vault, as set forth in your said proposal, the amount being deemed reasonable and a public exigency requiring the immediate performance of the work.

Payment will be made after the satisfactory completion of the work by you and its acceptance by the Government, from the appropriation for Mint Building, Denver, Colorado.

Respectfully,

Supervising Architect.

# Master Builders' Association

**OF DENVER, COLORADO.**

213 AND 214 CONTINENTAL BUILDING,
COR. 16TH AND LAWRENCE STS.
'PHONE MAIN 682.

Denver, Colo., April 14 1905.

To Mr Henrich U.S. Mint
Denver.

Will put one course of hot pitch over entire surface (roof of sweep cellar) on present concrete, then lay #25 tarred felt 2 ply, mopped solid, then another coat of hot pitch, on top of this will lay 3 ply of #25 tarred felt mopped solid, then finally put on a coat of hot pitch over entire surface. Make edges joining and flashing tight, and guarantee the work to be waterproof. Remove soil and replace same, (soil to be moved only to space adjoining cellar) for the sum of $272.00

respectfully Jno Gregor

The Supervising Architect,

Washington, D.C.

Dear Sir:-

I hereby submit proposal to repair the roof of sweeps cellar new mint, Denver, as follows:-

Remove sod and dirt; put on good coat of plaster sufficient to make smooth surface on concrete arches, and cover with four ply heavy tar paper turned up at edges to the grade of lawn, north end to extend four feet outside of wall line for drainage; cover paper with good coat of pitch; replace dirt and level off. The job to be guaranteed for one year from date of completion., for the consideration of Four Hundred Sixty Dollars ($460.)

A. Morrell.
Contractor & Builder.

#630 17th St.,
Denver, Colo.

45
36
270
135
1620

Cost about

DENVER NEW MINT

M

IN REPLYING QUOTE UPPER INITIAL, RIGHT HAND CORNER.

TREASURY DEPARTMENT

WASHINGTON Oct. 17, 1904.

Custodian,

U. S. Mint, (New),

Denver, Colo.

Sir:

The Department has this day authorized Mr. J. M. Mossman, #72 Maiden Lane, New York, N. Y., to clean, repair when necessary, and guarantee their proper working during the fiscal year ending June 30, 1905, of the five time locks attached to vault doors in the building in your custody, at a cost of $10.00 each.

It is understood that Mr. Mossman's representative will be in Denver on his regular trip about next May. After he cleans these locks and hands to you the guarantees for the same, you are authorized to issue a voucher for the expense and to forward it here for payment from the appropriation for "Vaults, Safes & Locks for Public Buildings, 1905."

Respectfully,

JK

Supervising Architect.

of U.S. designated
to guarantee proper
working of 5 timer
locks on vaults at
Denver Mint, during
fiscal yr. 1905.

TO THE USERS OF . . . .

# THE DIEBOLD TIME LOCKS.

In view of our guarantee for "the proper working" of our TIME LOCKS, which requires that "at your expense" they shall "be examined, cleaned, and if necessary, repaired once a year by an expert to be designated by us," we have appointed MR. J. M. MOSSMAN, No. 72 Maiden Lane, New York, our General Agent, to clean, oil and otherwise care for Time Locks of our manufacture.

Experts bearing proper credentials from Mr. Mossman, will be entitled to fill all requirements the same as if sent directly from us.

Very Respectfully,

Diebold Safe & Lock Co.

(Ed. 1-18-1904—1,000,000.)

No. 1767. TREASURY DEPARTMENT

C. A. Farr

6/22/05

**Mossman Co.,**

ive Agents for the cleaning of the

# LD TIME LOCKS

THE UNITED STATES.

[redacted] 72 MAIDEN LANE.

NEW YORK, MAY 1 1905

~~Mr.~~ Custodian

~~Cashier~~ U. S. Mint

Denver Col.

DEAR SIR:

Permit us to call your attention to the fact that to prevent the lapsing of the guaranty of your DIEBOLD TIME LOCK, it is necessary that it shall be examined, cleaned (and repaired if necessary) once each year by an expert to be designated or approved by us.

We beg to state that our expert, Mr. C. A. FARR. will be in your vicinity on or about the 2nd of June and will call upon you prepared to inspect and clean your device. If you decide not to employ our expert, but to assume the responsibility yourselves, we will then thank you to notify us by return mail, thus avoiding the expense of his calling upon you.

For the thorough examination and cleaning of the DIEBOLD TIME LOCK we make a fixed charge of $10.00. The examination, if properly made now, will continue the guaranty in effect for another year, and it is to your interest, even more than ours, to have your Timer properly inspected at regular intervals, inasmuch as your neglecting to do this releases us from our guaranty.

In addition to this we beg you will at all times promptly inform us of any irregularity in the working of your Time Lock, or any difficulty which you may experience in its use.

Before admitting our expert, that you may know he is the man we send, please compare his signature, as he shall write it for you, with that in the corner below.

After inspecting and cleaning your Timer he will furnish a printed receipt for his charges, as evidence of the fact that the Timer has been examined and adjusted in such a manner as to continue our guaranty in effect for another year.

Yours very respectfully,

J M Mossman [redacted]

Signature

President.

SAFE AND LOCK CO.

DENVER, NEW MINT
Q

OFFICE OF SUPERVISING ARCHITECT

IN REPLYING, QUOTE UPPER INITIAL, RIGHT HAND CORNER.

TREASURY DEPARTMENT

WASHINGTON, April 27, 1905.

The Custodian,

New Mint,

Denver, Colorado.

Sir:

Referring to the statements contained in your communication of February 25th, last, in relation to the condition of the wood floor in the Adjusting Room in the building in your custody, you are advised that the matter received the attention of Mr. A. A. Packard, Inspector of Public Buildings, during his recent visit to the building, and from the statements made in his report it is very doubtful as to whether a new floor would not in a short time develop cracks and become as unsatisfactory as the one now in place.

Mr. Packard's report was submitted to the Director of the Mint, who decided after conference that his Bureau would furnish a carpet for the floor, which could be removed at stated intervals and burned and a new carpet supplied in lieu thereof. For this reason, therefore, it has been decided by the Office to consider only such minor repairs to the present floor as will make it tight and place it in condition as a body for the carpet, and you are requested to prepare a brief specification for correcting the conditions in the present floor, if such work is necessary, and, based thereon, to secure and forward two or more competitive bids for the work, with your specific recommendation as to acceptance. Please accompany the bids by a copy of the specification, and keep the expense involved as small as possible.

A copy of this letter has been transmitted to the Director of the Mint for his information.

Respectfully,

L
Elsh

Supervising Architect.

DENVER, NEW MINT
Q

OFFICE OF SUPERVISING ARCHITECT

IN REPLYING, QUOTE UPPER INITIAL, RIGHT HAND CORNER.

TREASURY DEPARTMENT

5

WASHINGTON, April 28, 1905. Jan

The Custodian,

New Mint,

Denver, Colorado.

Sir:

Referring to your communication of the 22d instant, transmitting two proposals for relaying certain cement floors at the building in your custody, and to Department letter of this day, notifying you of the acceptance of the proposal of The Hinchman-Renton Fire Proofing Company, you are advised that the certified check which accompanied the bid of Charles Heimbecker will be returned to him directly by the Office.

Respectfully,

Supervising Architect.

DENVER NEW MINT.
V.

OFFICE OF SUPERVISING ARCHITECT

IN REPLYING QUOTE UPPER INITIAL, RIGHT HAND CORNER.

TREASURY DEPARTMENT

WASHINGTON April 27,1905.

Inclosure 5102.

The Custodian,
U. S. Mint (New),
Denver, Colorado.

Sir:

Inclosed find copy of a report of the 21st instant, as the result of a recent examination of the floor of the Sweeps cellar at the building in your custody, and as soon as the defect noted therein is remedied, you are requested to advise the office with your specific recommendation, in order that the proceeds of the check of the contractor may be returned to him.

Respectfully,

Supervising Architect.

UNITED STATES MINT

Denver, Colo., April 21st, 1905.

Supervising Architect,

Washington, D.C.

Sir:-

Following instructions in Department letter "S", under date of April 4th, I have made an inspection of the cement floor of the Sweeps Cellar, originally defective, and find that it has been satisfactorily repaired. Practically the entire floor has been relaid and given a grade of at least three inches from the side walls to the dry wells, but there is still a slight place in the center between the two dry wells which does not drain properly. The sub-contractor has been informed in regard to this defect, and as soon as this matter is satisfactorily remedied, I would recommend that general contractor be relieved from further responsibility regarding this matter.

Respectfully,

Allyn A. Packard,

Inspector Public Buildings.

DENVER, NEW MINT

Q

THE SUPERVISING ARCHITECT

IN REPLYING QUOTE UPPER INITIAL, RIGHT HAND CORNER

Inclosure 5219

TREASURY DEPARTMENT

OFFICE OF THE SECRETARY

WASHINGTON, April 26, 1905.

The Custodian,

U. S. Mint (New),

Denver, Colorado.

Sir:

Inclosed find copy of a report submitted to the Department under date of the 19th instant by Mr. A. A. Packard, Inspector of Public Buildings, as the result of a further examination of the cement floors in the building in your custody, and there is also transmitted copy of a Department letter this day addressed to The Hinchman-Renton Fire Proofing Company, accepting their bid, which was transmitted in your letter of the 22d instant, for relaying the floors in the melting and coining rooms.

Your attention is called to the fact that in the performance of the work it will be necessary to adjust twelve outlet electric light boxes in the coining room, and in accordance with the recommendations in the report, and in view of the public exigency which requires the immediate performance of the work, you are hereby authorized to incur an expenditure not to exceed seventy-five dollars ($75.00) for the labor and material incident to adjusting the boxes, it being believed that the Electrician on duty at the building can supervise this work in order to secure satisfactory results, and upon its completion forward vouchers to the Supervising Architect, duly certified and receipted in the usual manner, and itemized as to the labor and material involved, for payment from the appropriation for "Repairs and Preservation of Public Buildings, 1905."

Your attention is particularly called to the inclosed copy of the letter accepting the bid for relaying the floors, and when the contract and bond have been approved by the Department, you will be advised, and you are requested to supervise the work, which is to be completed within twenty days from the date of such approval, in order that the results desired may be attained.

You are also requested, upon satisfactory completion of the work, to advise the Supervising Architect to that effect, in order that, should an examination of the same be desired by a representative, such can be made, and you will then forward vouchers in payment, in accordance with the acceptance, duly certified and receipted in the usual manner, for payment from the appropriation for "Repairs and Preservation of Public Buildings, 1905."

It is also requested that, after the lapse of a reasonable time, should it develop that the floors in the melting and coining rooms have proved satisfactory, you will secure and forward, based upon the specifications which formed the basis of the present acceptance, proposals for relaying the floors in the whitening, rolling, and cutting rooms, and the private corridor connecting the same, which it is believed will complete the defective cement floors in the building. These bids should be accompanied by your specific recommendation as to acceptance, and it is to be understood that a guarantee of three years is to be given for such floors.

Please acknowledge the receipt of this letter.

Respectfully,

Acting Secretary.

DENVER, NEW MINT
Q

THE SUPERVISING ARCHITECT

IN REPLYING, QUOTE UPPER INITIAL, RIGHT HAND CORNER

TREASURY DEPARTMENT

OFFICE OF THE SECRETARY

WASHINGTON, April 28, 1905.

The Kinchman-Benton Fire Proofing Company,

1815 Arapahoe Street,

Denver, Colorado.

Sirs:

In view of the public exigency which requires the immediate performance of the work, and Departmental approval, your proposal of the 20th instant, submitted to the Supervising Architect by the Custodian of the New Mint at Denver, Colorado, in his letter of the 22d instant, and being deemed the better of the two bids for the reason that you agree to perform the work in accordance with the specifications, is hereby accepted in the sum of twelve hundred and fifty dollars ($1,250.00) for relaying cement floors in the Melting and Coining Rooms at the building named, in strict accordance with the specifications upon which your proposal was based and such instructions as may be given to you by the Custodian or other representative of the Government detailed to examine and report upon the work.

It is to be understood and agreed that this acceptance is to be based upon the following conditions:

That you are to execute a formal contract, with bond in the sum of one thousand dollars ($1,000.00), guaranteeing the faithful performance of the work embraced in this acceptance, a form for which will be forwarded. This contract, with bond, must be executed in strict accordance with the rules printed at the head of such form, and be returned to the Supervising Architect of this Department at once;

That said contract and bond will also guarantee the floors and expansion joints to be free from cracks for a period of three years from the completion of the work and payment therefor;

That the work is to be completed within twenty days from the date of approval of said contract and bond, of which you will be advised by wire;

That the brand of cement used in the work shall meet with the approval of the Supervising Architect of this Department before being applied, and in order that delay may be avoided, it is requested that samples of both the "Iola" and "Ideal" Portland cements, as stated in your proposal, be submitted by you to the Supervising Architect for approval; said samples to contain a sufficient quantity of the cement to enable satisfactory tests to be made, and in forwarding the samples you should accompany the same by a letter of transmittal, giving the name of the brand proposed to be used by you in connection with the work;

That either hot asphalt or "gilsonite" will be allowed for use in filling the expansion joints in accordance with the specifications, you to specify which you will use; it being understood that such joints are to be embraced in the guarantee to be given by you as being free from cracks for a period of three years;

That upon satisfactory completion of the work and acceptance by the Department, payment therefor will be made from the appropriation for "Repairs and Preservation of Public Buildings, 1906."

Acknowledge the receipt of this letter.

Respectfully,

(Signed) H. A. Taylor,

Acting Secretary.

UNITED STATES MINT BUILDING,

Denver, Colo., April 19, 1905.

Supervising Architect,

Washington, D.C.

Sir:-

Following instructions in Department letter "S" under date of April 4th, I visited Denver, Colorado, and have made a further investigation relative to the repairing or remedying defects in the cement floors in certain rooms in the building.

In my former report, under date of January 24, 1905, relative to this matter, I stated that "If it was deemed advisable to repair these floors in such a way that reliable and responsible contractors will guarantee permanent results free from cracks, I offer the following specifications for the work, which I understand will receive such a guarantee". - Upon investigating this matter again, and interviewing several specialists in this line of work, I find nearly as many different opinions as men interviewed, and when experts disagree the layman is somewhat at sea as to the wisest method to pursue. One party claims it will be impossible under any specifications to lay a floor that will not crack at least in the joints or partitions between the blocks, and another party, with as good a reputation and as much experience, claims that it can be done, and a third party claims it can be done. Inasmuch as there is such a variance of opinion in regard to this matter, amongst those supposed to be best informed, I believe it will be wise at present to only attempt to repair two of these rooms, namely, the coining room, which is the largest of the rooms in question and the one in which the floor is in the worst condition and the one to which the original and most serious objection was made, also the floor in the melting room, 1st floor.

The coining room also affords conditions most difficult to overcome, and if successful results can be obtained here, the remedying of defects in the other rooms can be undertaken later with more surety of success.

After considering the various statements made by different contractors, I have compiled a specification which meets the approval of the majority of men interviewed, and which will receive a three year guarantee that the floors will be free from cracks except in expansion joints which are to be filled with asphalt or some water-proof and pliable material.

As the new work contemplates raising the floors about one and one half inches, it will be necessary to adjust 12 outlet electric light boxes in the coining room, and as this work, although not difficult, must be carefully and accurately done, I would recommend that it be eliminated from the general contract and assigned to the electrician in charge of work at the mint under the Custodian's charge, and that he be allowed or authorized to expend, for additional help and necessary materials, a sum not to exceed $75.

The work in the two rooms, as specified, I estimate should not cost to exceed about $1700., and would recommend that it be undertaken as soon as satisfactory and responsible bids can be obtained.

I enclose herewith a specification for the work, and have given a copy to the Custodian in order that he may obtain bids and forward to the Department for approval, as I understand they are expecting to install machinery in these rooms shortly and are desirous of having this work attended to as soon as possible.

Respectfully,

Allyn A. Packard,

Inspector of Public Buildings.

C. ...HEFLER, Prest and Mgr. N. C. FISHER, Sec'y and Treas.

THE GARDEN CITY SAND CO.

SUITE 1201-1206 SECURITY BUILDING,

FIFTH AVE & MADISON STS.

CHICAGO.

TELEPHONES: MAIN 4827. AUTO. 8827.

Chicago, May 2, 1905.

Mr. F. N. Downer,

Custodian, New Mint,

Denver, Colo.

Dear Sir:-

Mr. A. A. Packard, Architect of this City, informs us that you are desirous of dampproofing a "sweep" room which is covered with 3ft. of lawn. We are in position to do this if our specifications are adhered to and a faithful and continuous coat of "R.I.W." is applied. If there is much evidence of seepage and the water is droping, we would suggest the removal of earth above the roof and flooding of same with "Marine Cement", which is absolutely without pores and through which water cannot pass. apply neat coat Portland cement then Replace the earth and then remove the cement plaster on the ceiling, which we understand from Mr. Packard is soft and falling off. On the concrete cement apply one good coat of "R.I.W." #232. In 24 hours, or any time suitable after application, put your finish coat of plaster (any kind) and you will never be troubled again with moisture.

Are the walls and floor dry? If not, a coat of "R.I.W." #232 will make them so. If you wish to paint the walls, #15 would be the proper material to use, as it dries hard and rapidly to receive oil paint, water paint, whitewash, etc..

If the conditions herein are followed, Toch Bros. of New York, the manufacturers of "R.I.W." Damp Resisting Compounds, will guarantee results. We beg to enclose "red book" and literature, which explains itself and hoping to hear from you favorably, we remain ;

**CIRCULAR LETTER.**

OFFICE OF SUPERVISING ARCHITECT

IN REPLYING, QUOTE UPPER INITIAL, RIGHT HAND CORNER

TREASURY DEPARTMENT

**ENCLOSURE**

WASHINGTON May 4, 1905.

The Custodian,

Sir:

Enclosed you will find instructions in regard to the care and operation of elevators in the building in your custody. You are requested to give the instructions to the elevator conductors or others in charge of the apparatus, and strict attention must be given to the same. Reports must be made regularly to you which must be transmitted to this office for such action as may be necessary.

You are requested to acknowledge the receipt of this letter.

Respectfully,

Supervising Architect.

INSTRUCTIONS IN REGARD TO THE CARE AND

OPERATION OF ELEVATORS.

May 4, 1905.

1. Especial attention is called to the fact that all parts of the elevator must be kept CLEAN.

2. All cables must be carefully examined at least once per month for broken wires, strands or other defects.

3. The machine must be inspected and one round trip made each day by the conductor before any passengers are allowed in the car; during this test trip the automatic terminal stop mechanism should be tested, and, if possible, the fireman or engineer should watch the operation of the machine while test trip is being made.

4. The conductor must close the entrance door to elevator before starting car, and must take every precaution to reduce the possibility of accident to zero.

5. All wire cables of the elevator must be given a coat of raw linseed oil and plumbago once per month.

6. The slide strips of elevator car and counterbalance weights must be cleaned once per month, and then greased.

7. When electric passenger elevators are in service, the conductor must stop at the floor at which the last passenger is delivered, and there await his next call.

8. During severe electrical storms, electric passenger elevators operated by current not generated within the building should be shut down, and the main switch or circuit breaker thrown out.

9. Any defects in the cables, safety devices, etc., of the elevator which may impair its safety or satisfactory operation must be immediately reported in writing to the Custodian.

DENVER NEW MINT

M

OFFICE OF SUPERVISING ARCHITECT

IN REPLYING, QUOTE UPPER INITIAL, RIGHT HAND CORNER.

TREASURY DEPARTMENT

F

WASHINGTON May 9, 1905.

Custodian,

U. S. Mint (New),

Denver, Colo.

Sir:

In reply to inquiry contained in your letter of the 4th instant, you are informed that in the opinion of this office all the time locks in the building in your custody should be cleaned and overhauled by Mr. Mossman's representative when he calls, in order to insure their satisfactory operation when placed in service.

Respectfully,

J K Taylor
Supervising Architect.

L.

DENVER NEW MINT.
V.

OFFICE OF SUPERVISING ARCHITECT

IN REPLYING QUOTE UPPER INITIAL RIGHT HAND CORNER

TREASURY DEPARTMENT

WASHINGTON May 8, 1905.

The Custodian,
New Mint,
Denver, Colorado.

Sir:

Under date of the 1st instant, The Hinchman-Renton Fire Proofing Company, the contractors for laying the new cement floors in the Coining and Melting rooms, at the building in your custody, state that they prefer to use Iola cement, incident to the work, and under separate cover there was received a small sample of the material.

The contractors have been wired this day that the office has no objection to the use of Iola cement, subject to the guarantee provisions of the contract, and you are requested to see that the cement is delivered at the building in unbroken and original packages, and you are requested to forward a quart sample of the cement so delivered, in order that it may be tested by this office.

Respectfully,

Supervising Architect.

DENVER, NEW MINT.
V.

TREASURY DEPARTMENT,

Washington, May 19, 1905.

Custodian,
U. S. Mint (New),
Denver, Colorado.

Sir:

By and with approval of the Department, under date of the 18th instant, and, in view of the statement contained in your letter of the 13th instant, and the public exigency which requires the immediate delivery of the article or performance of the work, you are hereby authorised to incur an expenditure not to exceedfive dollars ($5.00), for repairs to packing threshold of outer door to storage vault in basement at the building in your custody.

Upon satisfactory completion of the work, forward voucher therefor, duly certified and receipted in the usual manner, for payment from the appropriation for "Vaults, Safes and Locks for Public Buildings, 1905".

Respectfully,

[signature]

Chief Executive Officer.

POSTAL TELEGRAPH — COMMERCIAL CABLES

CLARENCE H. MACKAY, PRESIDENT.

# TELEGRAM

REGISTERED TRADE-MARK. DESIGN PATENT NO. 36369.

The Postal Telegraph-Cable Company (Incorporated) transmits and delivers this message subject to the terms and conditions printed on the back of this blank.

*Received at Main Office, 920 17th Street, Ernest & Cranmer Building, Denver.* (TELEPHONES 4500, 4501)

230-ch [illegible] 27-Govt, [illegible]:31pm

Washington, D.C., May 20-05

Custodian New Mint,

Denver, Colo.

Floor in melting room must be laid in four blocks specification must be strictly complied with.

C. E. Kemper, Acting Supervising Architect

---

POSTAL TELEGRAPH — COMMERCIAL CABLES

CLARENCE H. MACKAY, PRESIDENT.

# TELEGRAM

628

REGISTERED TRADE-MARK. DESIGN PATENT NO. 36369.

The Postal Telegraph-Cable Company (Incorporated) transmits and delivers this message subject to the terms and conditions printed on the back of this blank.

*Received at Main Office, 920 17th Street, Ernest & Cranmer Building, Denver.* (TELEPHONES 4500, 4501)

[illegible] CH. [illegible] 24 Govt

Washington DC. May [illegible]

[illegible] U. S. New Mint,

Denver, Colo.

[illegible] [illegible] Fireproofing Co [illegible]

C. [illegible],

[illegible]

DENVER, NEW MINT

Q

IN REPLYING QUOTE UPPER INITIAL RIGHT HAND CORNER

Inclosure 5184

TREASURY DEPARTMENT

WASHINGTON, May 24, 1905.

S

The Custodian,

New Mint,

Denver, Colorado.

Sir:

Referring to your communication of the 19th instant, and to Department telegram of this day, inclosed find copy of a letter this day addressed to The Hinchman-Renton Fire Proofing Company, accepting their proposal in the additional sum of $25.00 for supplying cove corner sub base in the Coining and Melting Rooms at the building in your custody, as an addition to their contract for relaying the cement floors in said rooms.

The inclosure will explain itself, and upon satisfactory completion of the work and acceptance by the Government, vouchers in accordance therewith should be certified by you for payment from the appropriation for "Repairs and Preservation of Public Buildings, 1905."

Respectfully,

[signature]

Acting Supervising Architect.

L

DENVER, NEW MINT

Q

THE SUPERVISING ARCHITECT

IN REPLYING QUOTE UPPER INITIAL, RIGHT HAND CORNER

TREASURY DEPARTMENT

OFFICE OF THE SECRETARY

WASHINGTON, May 24, 1905.

The Hinchman-Renton Fire Proofing Company,

1915 Arapahoe Street,

Denver, Colorado.

Sirs:

In view of the public exigency which requires the immediate performance of the work, your proposal of the 19th instant, addressed to the Supervising Architect of this Department and submitted by the Custodian of the new Mint at Denver, Colorado, in letter of the same date, is hereby accepted in the sum of twenty-five dollars for making cove corner sub base three inches high, one inch at top and two and one-half inches at base, to join floors now being laid under your contract in the Coining and Melting Rooms in the building named.

It is understood that the amount above named is to be in addition to that embraced in your present contract of $1,250.00 for relaying the cement floors in the rooms named, and that the work is to be of the character called for by the specifications which form the basis of said contract, and subject to the same guarantee.

It is understood and agreed that this acceptance is not to affect the time for completion of the work, as required by the terms of your contract; that the same is without prejudice to any and all rights of the United States thereunder; and is without prejudice also to any and all rights of the United States against the sureties on the bond executed for the faithful fulfillment of the contract.

A copy of this communication has been submitted to the Custodian of the building with directions to certify to vouchers in accordance therewith upon final completion of the work and its acceptance by the Government, from the appropriation for "Repairs and Preservation of Public Buildings, 1905."

Respectfully,

(Signed) J. B. Reynolds,

Acting Secretary.

TREASURY DEPARTMENT

WASHINGTON, May 25, 1905.

SUPERVISING ARCHITECT

IN REPLYING QUOTE UPPER INITIAL RIGHT HAND CORNER.

Inclosure 5191

The Custodian,

New Mint,

Denver, Colorado.

Sir:

Inclosed find copy of a report of the 20th instant, as the result of an inspection of the elevators at the building in your custody.

The report will explain itself, and you are advised that no change will be made in elevator No. 3 at the present time.

Respectfully,

[signature]

Acting Supervising Architect.

Office of the Custodian,

New Mint Building,

Denver, Colo., May 20th.1905

The Supervising Architect,

Treasury Department,

Washington, D.C.

Sir:

In compliance with Department orders L.A.S. dated May 11th. I have to report that I have inspected the elevators in this building, and have found over head gears, all cables, safety devices, controlling appliances and motors in good condition and properly adjusted.

In case of Elevator No. 1 the six months operating test will expire on July 6th.

In case of Elevator No. 3, which runs between the melting room and the weigh clerk room, the motor for which is located in an alcove just underneath the ceiling of the latter room, complaint was made that when this motor was running it caused considerable vibration and noise in the weigh clerk's room, seriously disturbing the needle of the weighing scale and interfering with the efficiency of the work in this room. I investigated this complaint and it seems to be well founded. The only practical way to eliminate this difficulty will be to either remove the motor to the basement, or, to install in the place of this elevator a direct hydraulic or pneumatic lift, and I recommend that a change be made when funds are available.

Respectfully,

Geo B Rice

Inspector M.&.E.Engineering.

T R E A S U R Y  D E P A R T M E N T,

Washington, June 2,1905.

The Supervising Architect,

Treasury Department.

Sir:-

Referring to your letter of recent date,relating to the floor of the adjusting room, U.S.Mint at Denver, I have to inform you that,in the opinion of this office,the cheaper and better way to remedy the defects in this wooden floor is to lay a thin floor on top of the present floor;the new floor to have as tight joints as possible to lay. If this recommendation is followed, the two swinging doors can be cut down and a higher threshold fitted under same.

(Signed) Geo.E.Roberts,

Director of the Mint.

DENVER, NEW MINT

[illegible]

Inclosure #124

TREASURY DEPARTMENT

WASHINGTON, June 5, 1905.

The Custodian,

New Mint,

Denver, Colorado.

Sir:

Inclosed find a communication, dated the 2d instant, from the Director of the Mint, in relation to laying the floor in the Adjusting Room at the building in your custody.

The inclosure will explain itself, and you are requested to prepare a brief specification for the work as indicated therein, and to secure and forward bids based upon the specifications with your specific recommendation as to acceptance.

Please return the inclosed letter with the bids, together with a copy of the specifications governing the work.

Upon receipt of the proposals, the matter will receive prompt attention.

Respectfully,

[signature]

Supervising Architect.

[illegible]

[illegible]

Denver, Colo.

Dear Sir:-

[illegible]

[illegible] across [illegible] pitch [illegible]

[illegible] surface [illegible]

[illegible] Will also remove [illegible]

[illegible] work is completed. [illegible]

[illegible] from [illegible]

[illegible]

[illegible]

[illegible]

[illegible] Co.

By [illegible]

[illegible]

.. course of construction for

in the building in your cust

instant, it appears that the

d by the 20th instant and the

e 15th or 20th proximo.

Upon the complete installation

office to that effect, stating

accordance with the contract

this Department in regard to

nt. Also state in your letter

nment has sustained any loss

act ...... the completion of

Custodian,
U. S. Mint (new),
Denver, Colorado.

Sir:

In accordance with the approval of the Department and in view of the statements contained in your letter of the [illegible] instant that the contractor refuses to perform the work, Department letter of [illegible] ultimo authorizing you to accept the proposal of John Graeger in amount two hundred seventy-two dollars ([illegible]), for repairing the roof of the sweeps cellar at the building in your custody, is hereby revoked; and you are now authorized to accept the proposal of The Hinchman-Renton Fire Proofing Company, in amount three hundred forty-two dollars ($342.00), for repairing the roof of the sweeps cellar as specified, the public exigency requiring the immediate performance of the work.

Give the work your personal supervision and upon satisfactory completion submit a voucher in duplicate for the expense, charged against the appropriation for "Repairs and Preservation of Public Buildings, 1906."

It is one of the conditions that the liability herein granted must be incurred before the 30th instant, and the work must be commenced before the expiration of the present fiscal year; otherwise this authority becomes void and of no effect. It should be understood also, that the work must be uninterruptedly carried to completion after commencement.

DENVER, NEW MINT
Q

OFFICE OF SUPERVISING ARCHITECT

IN REPLYING, QUOTE UPPER INITIAL RIGHT HAND CORNER.
Inclosure 7850

TREASURY DEPARTMENT

WASHINGTON, June 30, 1905.

The Custodian,

New Mint,

Denver, Colorado.

Sir:

There is transmitted herewith, copy of a report of the 23d instant as the result of an examination of cement floors in the building in your custody.

The report will explain itself, and upon receipt of the proposals for the new floors contemplated, consideration will be given thereto, and in your letter transmitting the bids please request authority to expend $125.00 for adjusting the floor boxes, as recommended in the report, so that this matter may be handled at the time the bids are being considered.

Respectfully,

L
Foote

J. K. Taylor
Supervising Architect.

The Supervising Architect,

Treasury Department.

Sir:-

Following instructions in Department letter "S", under date of June 9th, I visited Denver, Colo., on June 21st and made an inspection of work under contract with The Hinchman-Renton Fire Proofing Co. for relaying cement floors in certain rooms.

The work has been practically completed for the last two or three weeks, except the cleaning off of wet sand and filling in of the joints with hot asphalt.

This work is being done now, and as soon as it has been completed to the satisfaction of the Custodian, I would recommend the payment of vouchers.

As far as physical appearances go, this work has been unusually well done, and I understand from Custodian and his assistant that the specifications were faithfully carried out.

In regard to the "bevel" referred to in my letter of instructions I desire to state that my specification called for "a slight bevel all around the room (this word room should have been "rooms") extending out about 18" from the line of the present base; also in the coining room a slight bevel at the three entrance doors, to allow the doors to swing properly". This wording appears to be a little misleading on account of the ambiguity of "as" in the word room, as it was my intention to have the bevel around the walls in the dining room as well as in the waiting room, but the reason for not specifying or desiring the bevel at the floors in the waiting room was on account of the difference of level of the original floor in the waiting room which was from one inch to one inch and a half lower than the adjoining corridor floor, the object of which was to permit the placing of the metal strips not referred to, a fact I did not understand at the time.

The real reason for the 1½" bevel around the walls of room was to preserve the original cement molding base which at the time of my inspection appeared to be in good condition and not necessary of removal.

ferred to.

With regard to the relaying of the balance of the cement floors on the main floor, namely in the Whitening, Rolling and Cutting rooms, adjoining corridor and Transfer room, I desire to state that at the time of my report of April 19th, 1905, was written, I deemed that a reasonable time should elapse after the completion of the floors in the coining and melting rooms before a proper judgment as to their success could be ascertained.

Inasmuch as the minting operations probably will not commence here for two or three months, and as the removing of the old and relaying of the new floors after the minting operations commence would be a source of great annoyance and inconvenience, I think the time limit for a proper judgment, as intended in my original report, could be waived and the new floors put down during the next month or two, as the floors just laid have a much better appearance now than the original floors had immediately after they were completed.

I have therefore prepared a specification for the necessary work, and instructed the Custodian to get bids as requested and forward them to the Department for approval as suggested, and I enclose herewith a copy of said specification.

As I deem the raising of these floors as necessary as those just finished, it will be necessary to adjust a number of outlet boxes and other boxes and plates, and I think the outlet boxes can be more properly adjusted under the supervision of the electrician at the mint, so I would therefore eliminate this work from the general contract and recommend that the Custodian be authorized to expend not to exceed $125.00 for this work.

I estimate that the expense of relaying the floors of the Whitening room, Rolling and Cutting room, Transfer room and the corridor between the melting room and coining room should not exceed $1000.00, and would recommend that it be undertaken in time to be satisfactorily completed on or before September 1st, 1905.

Respectfully,

Allyn A. Packard,

Inspector, Public Buildings.

# POSTAL TELEGRAPH COMMERCIAL CABLES

CLARENCE H. MACKAY, PRESIDENT.

# TELEGRAM

5505

The Postal Telegraph-Cable Company (Incorporated) transmits and delivers this message subject to the terms and conditions printed on the back of this blank.

*Received at Main Office, 920 17th Street, Ernest & Cranmer Building, Denver. (Telephones 4500, 4501.)*

95.ks.cn.n.31.gov't 320p

Washington,DC.June 24-5

Custodian,

New Mint, Denver,Colo.

Accept proposal Hinchman renton fire proofing .Co amount three hundred forty two dollars for repairing roof of sweeps cellar letter follows.

C H Keep,Asst Secy.

KONKERIT"

COATING FOR

**OUTSIDE.**

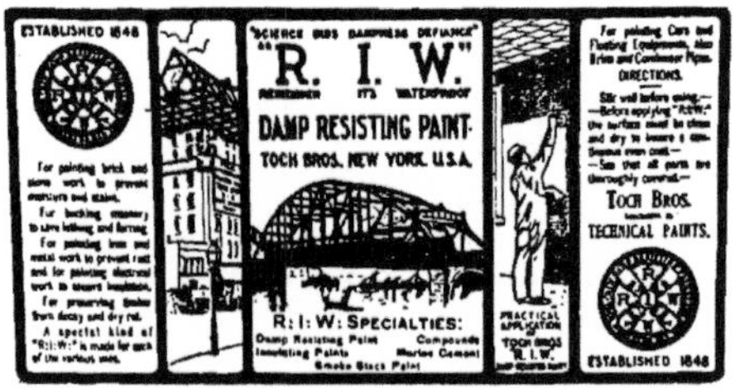


"KONKERIT"

COATING FOR

OUTSIDE.

Telephone, 568 Spring
468 – 470 – 472 WEST BROADWAY NEW YORK

REPRESENTED BY
C. B. SHEFLER, Pres. & Mgr. N. C. FISHER, Sec'y & Treas.
**THE GARDEN CITY SAND CO.**
SUITE 1201-1206 SECURITY BUILDING
Fifth Avenue and Madison St. CHICAGO, ILL.
TELEPHONE, MAIN 4827

July 22nd, 1905.

F. N. Downer,

Custodian, New Mint,

Denver, Colorado.

Dear Sir,

We beg to refer you to our letter of May 2nd, and to subsequent correspondence relative to waterproofing of your sweep room in the New Mint. Have you abandoned the project, or are you still open for negotiations? We will be glad to take the matter up with you if you wish us to, and await your reply.

Respectfully yours,

THE GARDEN CITY SAND CO.

Gordon Douglas.

DENVER, NEW MINT
Q

OFFICE OF SUPERVISING ARCHITECT

IN REPLYING QUOTE UPPER INITIAL, RIGHT HAND CORNER

Inclosure 7757

TREASURY DEPARTMENT

WASHINGTON, July 22, 1905.

The Custodian,

U. S. Mint (New),

Denver, Colorado.

Sir:

In connection with your letter of the 13th instant in relation to this matter, please find inclosed a copy of a letter this day addressed to The Macneale & Urban Company in regard to the safe ordered from them for the building in your custody.

Respectfully,

J K Taylor
Supervising Architect.

L
JUCh

DENVER, NEW MINT
Q

OFFICE OF SUPERVISING ARCHITECT

IN REPLYING, QUOTE UPPER INITIAL, RIGHT HAND CORNER.

TREASURY DEPARTMENT

WASHINGTON, July 12, 1905.

The Macneale & Urban Company,

Hamilton,

Ohio.

Sirs:

Information has been received from the Custodian of the U. S. Mint at Denver, Colorado, to the effect that the safe ordered from you for the Assay Weigh Room has been delivered in an unsatisfactory condition; that is, the exterior painting has been badly scarred in places, the boltwork on the doors does not operate satisfactorily, and the hinge tips are not finished in a first-class and workmanlike manner.

It is requested that you will immediately take the proper steps to have this safe completed as provided for in your agreement.

Respectfully,

(Signed) J. K. Taylor,

Supervising Architect.

DENVER, NEW MINT

OFFICE OF SUPERVISING ARCHITECT

IN REPLYING, QUOTE UPPER INITIAL, RIGHT HAND CORNER

TREASURY DEPARTMENT

S

WASHINGTON, July 19, 1905.

The Custodian,

U. S. Mint (New),

Denver, Colorado.

Sir:

Referring to your communication of the 12th instant, transmitting bids for the laying of a new wood floor in the Adjusting Room at the building in your custody, you are advised that the amounts are deemed to be far in excess of what a fair estimate of the cost of the work justifies, and before further action is taken you are requested to advise this Office as to whether there are such unusual conditions in connection with the laying of the floor, the price of the lumber, etc., as to cause the amounts of the bids to be as large as those furnished.

Respectfully,

J. K. Taylor
Supervising Architect.

DENVER, NEW MINT.

THE SUPERVISING ARCHITECT

IN REPLYING QUOTE UPPER INITIAL
RIGHT HAND CORNER

TREASURY DEPARTMENT

OFFICE OF THE SECRETARY

WASHINGTON July 15, 1905.

Enclosure 4529.

The Custodian,
U.S.Mint (New),
Denver, Colorado.

Sir:

Enclosed find copy of a Department letter this day addressed to The Hinchman-Renton Fire Proofing Company, of your city, accepting their proposal in the sum of eighteen hundred and eighty-six dollars ($1,886.00), for relaying cement floors in the Whitening, Rolling and Cutting and Transfer rooms and the connecting corridor, at the building in your custody, based upon certain conditions, which are particularly called to your attention.

You will be furnished with a copy of the contract when approved by the Department, and you are requested to give the work your supervision to see that it is executed strictly in accordance with the terms of the contract, and when the cement is delivered at the building, to see that it is in unbroken packages, with name of brand and maker stamped thereon, and you will then forward to the Supervising Architect a two quart sample for test.

When the work is nearing completion, advise the Supervising Architect to that effect, in order that an inspection may be ordered, and upon satisfactory completion of the work, you are authorized to certify to voucher therefor, for payment from the appropriation "Repairs and Preservation of Public Buildings, 1906".

In connection with the above work, and in view of the approval of the Department, the statements and recommendations contained in your letter of the 5th instant, you are authorized to incur liabilities in a sum not to exceed one hundred and twenty-five dollars ($125.oo), for the labor and material necessary and incident to adjusting the outlet boxes and electrical conduits, when laying the cement floors in the rooms herein above noted, and upon satisfactory delivery of the materials and performance of the work, to forward vouchers for the expense, duly certified and receipted, in the usual manner, for payment from the appropriation "Repairs and Preservation of Public Buildings, 1906".

Acknowledge the receipt of this letter.

Respectfully,

Acting Secretary.

S.

T.

DENVER, NEW MINT.

THE SUPERVISING ARCHITECT

IN REPLYING QUOTE UPPER INITIAL RIGHT HAND CORNER

TREASURY DEPARTMENT

OFFICE OF THE SECRETARY

WASHINGTON July 15, 1905.

The Hinchman-Renton Fire Proofing Company,
1615 Arapahoe street,
Denver, Colorado.

Sirs:

In view of the public exigency which requires the immediate performance of the work, and Departmental approval, your proposal of the 29th ultimo, addressed to the Custodian, New Mint, Denver, Colorado, and transmitted by that official on the same date, is hereby accepted, in the sum of eighteen hundred and eighty-six dollars (1,886.00), for relaying cement floors in the Whitening, Rolling and Cutting and Transfer rooms, and the corridor adjacent to the rooms named and connecting the Coining and Melting rooms, in the building named, in strict accordance with the specifications upon which your bid was based and such instructions as may be given to you by the Custodian of the building or other representatives of the Government detailed to examine and report upon the work.

It is to be understood and agreed that this acceptance is to be based upon the following conditions:

That you are to execute a formal contract, with bond in the sum of fifteen hundred dollars ($1,500.00), to guarantee the faithful performance of the work embraced in this acceptance, a form for which will be forwarded. This contract, with bond, must be executed in strict accordance with the rules printed at the head of such form, and be returned to the Supervising Architect of this Department at

case. You will note from the rules indicated that solvent individual sureties will be acceptable to the Department.

That said contract and bond will also guarantee the floors and expansion joints to be free from cracks for a period of three years from the completion of the work and payment therefor.

That the work is to be completed within thirty (30) working days from the date of approval of said contract and bond, of which you will be advised by wire.

That the brand of cement to be used is the "Iola" Portland, as proposed by you, with the understanding that the cement is to be delivered at the building in unbroken packages, with the brand and makers name plainly marked thereon; tests to be made of the material delivered, from samples to be forwarded by the Custodian, to determine whether it is satisfactory to the Supervising Architect.

That upon satisfactory completion of the work, as herein specified, payment will be made from the appropriation "Repairs and Preservation of Public Buildings, 1906".

Acknowledge the receipt of this letter.

Respectfully,

(Signed) J B Reynolds
Acting Secretary.

S.
T.

Jnr Ctk L

**RECEIVED** at 1114 to 1118 17th St., Denver, Colo.

TELEPHONES MAIN 4444, 4445 AND 4446.

137amtm 25 paid govt

K Washington DC aug 5-1903

Custodian New Mint Denver, Col.

Notify Hinchman Renton Fireproofing Co their bond approved when will they commence work.

Jas A. Wetmore, Acting Chief Executive Officer

1209p

DENVER, NEW MINT
Q

OFFICE OF SUPERVISING ARCHITECT

IN REPLYING, QUOTE UPPER INITIAL, RIGHT HAND CORNER.

Inclosure 7260

TREASURY DEPARTMENT

S

WASHINGTON, August 12, 1905.

The Custodian,

U. S. Mint (New),

Denver, Colorado.

Sir:

Referring to your communications of the 12th and 25th ultimo, with proposals for laying a new floor in the Adjusting Room at the building in your custody, you are advised that the Office is in receipt of a communication from the Director of the Mint in which the statement is made that he will not consider the supply of linoleum for the floor, and further, that it will not be necessary to oil the floor, as the same will be covered by a cheap carpet, which can be burned after a sufficient length of time to permit of its being impregnated with filings.

It is also believed that less expense will be involved in the supply of a 7/8" thick floor, in lieu of 5/8", and as the bid submitted in your letter of the 28th ultimo, in the sum of $400.00, is not from one of the bidders who were in the original competition, it has been decided to reject the proposals transmitted, and to secure new competition.

The specification for the work, therefore, has been modified, and three copies of the same are herewith transmitted, and you are requested to secure three or more bids for the performance of the work in accordance therewith, the proposals to provide for the supply of either a 5/8" thick or a 7/8" thick floor at the option of the Office, and it being with the distinct understanding that the floor is to be extra tight and smooth.

In inviting the proposals, please have each bid accompanied by a certified check, in the sum of 10 per cent. of the amount thereof, to guarantee the faithful performance of the work, and you will also return with the proposals one of the specifications which are forwarded herewith.

Respectfully,

Supervising Architect.

DENVER MINT (NEW)
G.

OFFICE OF SUPERVISING ARCHITECT

IN REPLYING QUOTE UPPER INITIAL RIGHT HAND CORNER

TREASURY DEPARTMENT

WASHINGTON July 26, 1905.

The Custodian,

Mint Building (New),

Denver, Colorado.

Sir:-

Referring to contract with the Diebold Safe & Lock Company for deposit weigh clerk's vault door of the building in your custody, I have to advise you that the company has requested payment therefor, and in order that a proper reply may be made thereto I have to request from you a report thereon, showing whether or not the work has been properly installed and all defects therein remedied to your satisfaction; and as the work does not appear to have been completed within contract time you are also requested to state the date on which it was practically completed, the causes for the delay, and whether or not the Government has sustained any loss on account thereof.

Please give this matter your early attention.

Respectfully,

Jas. A. Wetmore
Acting Chief Executive Officer.

DENVER. NEW MINT.
B

OFFICE OF SUPERVISING ARCHITECT

IN REPLYING, QUOTE UPPER INITIAL, RIGHT HAND CORNER

TREASURY DEPARTMENT

WASHINGTON August 25, 1905.

Custodian,

U. S. Mint (new),

Denver, Colorado.

Sir:

Referring to your letter of the 16th instant, forwarding sample of "Iola Portland Cement" proposed to be used by the contractors for relaying cement floors in the Whitening, Rolling, and Cutting and Transfer rooms, and the connecting corridor, in the building in your custody, you are advised that the same is hereby approved for the work.

Respectfully,

Supervising Architect.

he Custodian,

U. S. Mint (New),

Denver, Colorado.

Sir:

There is transmitted herewith, copy of a report of June 24, last, submitted by Mr. A. A. Packard, Inspector of Publ[ic] Buildings, in relation to the supply of a fireproof curtain, coal-hole covers, and floors in unfinished rooms in the buil[ding] in your custody.

There is also submitted, copy of a letter addressed to [this] Office under date of the 6th instant by the Director of the M[int] to whom Mr. Packard's report was referred, and in view of the statements made therein it is not deemed necessary to supply [the] curtain, and no further action in this regard will be taken.

You are requested to give consideration to the question [of] heating the wall room, as suggested in the Director's letter, and to secure and forward bids for installing in this room a pipe coil or radiator containing 60 square feet of radiating surface; to be connected to nearest available steam flow and [re]turn piping in place; the supply to the coil or radiator to be provided with 1-1/4" radiator valve and return pipe with a 1/[2"] thermostatic valve, both valves to be of the same pattern as those now in place.

You will also note that no further action is necessary in connection with the supply of floors in the basement and in the strip annealing room in the attic, as these will be put in position by the Mint Bureau in connection with certain machinery to be installed by it.

Particular attention is called to the question of coal hole covers, and while it is noted that the Director objects to raising the level of the coping around these holes by reason of trouble in the handling of teams, yet it is thought that the same can be made tight by raising the curb as suggested, but also sloping the same so that it will not absolutely interfere with the wheels, riding over the top if necessary. If, however, it is your judgment that some other method can be adopted for making the covers tight, this should receive consideration, and proposals based upon the best method should be secured and submitted for the action of the Office.

In this connection, and referring to Office letter of this day, you will note that Mr. A. A. Packard, Inspector of Public Buildings, will again be in your city within a few days in connection with the cement floors now being laid, and it is suggested that while he is present a conference with him in regard to the features noted in this letter may be of service.

Respectfully,

Supervising Architect.

U.S.MINT, Denver, Colo., June 23, 1905.

The Supervising Architect,

Treasury Department.

Sir:-

With regard to the list of certain items of work which the Custodian desires to have done, referred to in Department letter under date of June 9th, 1905, I have taken up the matter of cement floors in balance of rooms on the first floor in a separate report, as Custodian was desirous of having that matter taken up independently of the other items.

The other matters named were:

1. Fireproof curtain between coal vault and boiler room.

2. Coal hole covers.

3. Floors in unfinished rooms, I have looked into and report as follows;

The curtain for the coal vault and boiler room is desired to keep out the dust and coal from being blown all over the engine room and boiler room. The coal used is a bituminous coal, containing a good deal of slack and when thrown into the vault draught carries the dust over the boilers and into the engine room. This could in my opinion be obviated to a certain extent if the coal was wet down before being thrown into the vaults A sheet iron curtain, however, would

[illegible]laims [illegible]

be more effective and also keep out the cold [illegible]

I find it [illegible] difficult to get any data in regard to [illegible]

are, and will have to defer this matter until I see the

catalogues or consult with parties in my headquarters.

[illegible] are not all [illegible] for that purpose, and

more than eight without raising them above the surface

[illegible] are set. Some of them are [illegible] [illegible] [illegible] to

[illegible] furnishing the greatest trouble consist of a pair of [illegible]

the [illegible] rooms, as they are directly over one of the [illegible]

It is essential that they should be water-tight, and this

[illegible] I think by raising them on a cement curb [illegible]

above the regular level.

[illegible] in the unfinished rooms in attic and basement are

necessary as any of the other rooms in the building when

operations commence, and I understand they were simply [illegible]

finishing contract on account of lack of funds.

[illegible] prepared a specification for the above work with the

of the sheet iron curtain, which I will take [illegible] and

that these repairs as specified should cost about $[illegible]

Apart, Fireproof curtains

Coal Hole coverings floors in

Unfurnished rooms

[illegible] we and also keep me

[illegible] difficult to get any d

[illegible] have to defer this mat

[illegible] variation in

[illegible]

[illegible] mixing the

[illegible]

[illegible] the greatest trouble and

ll because they are directly o

essential that they should be

that I think by raising them a

the regular level.

In the unfinished rooms in n

dry as any of the other rooms

are necessary, and - understand

ing contract on account of lack

passed a specification for the

[illegible]

been required as outlined above

Washington, D. C., August 8, 1905.

The Supervising Architect,

Washington, D. C.

Sir:-

Referring to the report of Inspector Packard of your office, in regard to the condition and changes sugested at the U. S. Mint building, Denver, Colorado, the correspondence being enclosed herewith, I have to say that the floors in basement and the floor of the Strip Annealing room, in the attic, were left in the present condition, not for lack of funds but for reasons given by this office, brought about by the fact that certain machines and pieces of apparatus were to be installed in the rooms in question and that this machinery had not been, in fact is not at this date finely decided upon. As this floor work has been held back at the request of this office it was thought proper to install same out of the appropriation under control of this office. If the floors were installed at this time we would have to cut them so much that they would be practically worthless; for that reason we will agree to place the floors in position at the time we are setting the machines that are going in the rooms in basement and in attic that are not now installed.

In regard to the coal hole covers I would consider it adviseable to put all covers in a serviceable condition but would consider it a mistake to raise the level of the coping around well holes as the teams would have trouble in turning.

The question of a curtain in the boiler room could be covered by the installation of a canvas fireproofed curtain; a metal curtain would be clumsy and in the way. The doors opening into the engine room and into stair case, are tin covered and are built so they will close automatically, if they work properly; for that reason the doors in question ought to remain closed at all times. Cold and severe weather in a boiler room is a fine quality, when boilers are being operated. In this connection I might say that it has been called to my attention that the well room was so cold, during last winter, that the water froze in the well tank; it would be a good idea to install a line of pipe heating coils, attached to side walls of the well room, to prevent freezing of water and air tank, as well as cylinders of compresors; in fact the well room should be heated.

Respectfully,

(Signed) Geo. E. Roberts,

Director of the Mint.

DENVER, NEW MINT

Q

OFFICE OF SUPERVISING ARCHITECT

IN REPLYING, QUOTE UPPER INITIAL, RIGHT HAND CORNER

TREASURY DEPARTMENT S

WASHINGTON, August 29, 1905.

The Custodian,

U. S. Mint (New),

Denver, Colorado.

Sir:

Referring to advices received from you, you are informed that Mr. A. A. Packard, Inspector of Public Buildings, in connection with other duties has been directed to visit the building in your custody and make an examination of work performed under an agreement with The Hinchman-Renton Fireproofing Company.

It is probable that Mr. Packard will be in Denver in three or four days after the receipt by you of this letter.

Respectfully,

J. K. Taylor
Supervising Architect.
JWG

DENVER, NEW MINT.
V.

OFFICE OF SUPERVISING ARCHITECT

IN REPLYING QUOTE UPPER INITIAL RIGHT HAND CORNER

TREASURY DEPARTMENT

WASHINGTON September 1, 1905.

The Custodian,
U. S. Mint (New),
Denver, Colorado.

Sir:

Your letter of the 18th ultimo, inclosing voucher for packing outer door of main storage vault in basement at the building in your custody, is received. This work was performed in accordance with Office letter addressed to you, under date of May 19th, last, in which you were authorized to forward vouchers in the sum of $5.00, payable from the appropriation for "Vaults, Safes and Locks for Public Buildings, 1905".

The work was performed subsequent to June 30, 1905, and falls as a charge against the same appropriation for the fiscal year, 1906.

The voucher has been amended in this respect, and proper entries made on the books of this Office, and a check for the amount will be forwarded, in your care.

Jas. A. [signature]
Acting Chief Executive Officer.

DENVER, NEW MINT
Q

OFFICE OF SUPERVISING ARCHITECT

IN REPLYING QUOTE UPPER INITIAL, RIGHT HAND CORNER

Inclosure 3522

TREASURY DEPARTMENT

WASHINGTON, Sept. 15, 1905.

The Custodian,

U. S. Mint (New),

Denver, Colorado.

Sir:

Inclosed find copy of a report of the 11th instant, as the result of an examination of work under the agreement with the Hinchman-Renton Fireproofing Company for relaying cement floors in certain rooms and halls at the building in your custody, from which you will note that the work, with the exception mentioned therein, has been entirely and satisfactorily completed.

When the Contractors have complied with the terms of their agreement in regard to filling the joints with gilsonite, you are requested to forward vouchers, duly certified and receipted, for consideration and payment.

Respectfully,

G

L 11/15th

Supervising Architect.

DENVER, COLO., U.S. MINT.

September 11th, 1908.

Supervising Architect,

Treasury Department.

Sir:-

In conformance with order in Department letter initial "A", [illegible] under date of August 28th, I visited Denver, Colorado on September [illegible] and made an inspection of the work under The Hitchcock-[illegible] Fireproofing Company, in sum of $[illegible], for relaying cement floors in certain rooms and halls on the first floor of the New Mint.

At the time of my visit the work had been completed, except the filling of the joints with the hot [illegible] cement.

The workmanship and general appearance of the floors are very satisfactory, and I understand the work has been carried out in strict accordance with the specifications and contract. The levels of the floors have been raised about 1-1/8", and I believe there will be no more trouble from cracks over plates or seams. The levels have been nicely adjusted at doorways and lower floors so that I believe no inconvenience will be experienced in using

Supervising Architect, 2.

The changing of electric pipes and outlet boxes has been done for a little less than the amount estimated, and I would recommend the payment of these vouchers also.

Respectfully,

Allyn A. Packard,

Inspector of Public Buildings.

DENVER, NEW MINT

Q

OFFICE OF SUPERVISING ARCHITECT

IN REPLYING QUOTE UPPER INITIAL RIGHT HAND CORNER

TREASURY DEPARTMENT S

WASHINGTON, Sept. 18, 1905.

The Custodian,

U. S. Mint (New),

Denver, Colorado.

Sir:

Referring to your communication of the 11th instant, reporting a broken hinge on the right-hand side of the steel flap of the bridge in the vestibule of vault "G" in the building in your custody, which, it is stated, is due to a defective casting, you are advised that, in the opinion of the Office, the Contractors for the installation of the work are responsible for this condition, and you should make demand upon them to repair the same without delay and without expense to the Government. It is not understood why they should demur to replacing a broken hinge due to a defective casting.

In the event, however, that, after a reasonable time, the Contractors fail to respond to your demand, please have the hinge repaired at an expense not to exceed $5.00, and forward voucher for the work for consideration and payment by the Department from the appropriation involved.

Respectfully,

Supervising Architect.

for such expression of views as he may desire to make.

Action on the proposals submitted by you for laying the floors in the room in question will be deferred until receipt of your reply to this letter.

Respectfully,

Supervising Architect.

DENVER, NEW MINT.

OFFICE OF SUPERVISING ARCHITECT

IN REPLYING, QUOTE UPPER INITIAL, RIGHT HAND CORNER.

TREASURY DEPARTMENT

WASHINGTON Sept. 29, 1905.

Custodian,
New Mint Building,
Denver, Colorado.

Sir:

Referring to your letter of August 22d in which you state that certain work covered by the accepted proposal of Mr. Joseph A. Seubert to change the level of the cement floor in the vault in the Deposit Weigh Clerk's room in the building in your custody, was found unnecessary, you are requested to consult with the contractor and advise this Office if there is any reason why the acceptance should not be revoked.

Respectfully,

[signature]

Acting Supervising Architect.

HM

# POSTAL TELEGRAPH COMMERCIAL CABLES

CLARENCE H. MACKAY, PRESIDENT.

# TELEGRAM

6 /

REGISTERED TRADE-MARK. DESIGN PATENT NO. 36369.



*Received at Main Office, 920 17th Street, Ernest & Cranmer Building, Denver.* (TELEPHONE 4800, 4801).



B"3Ch J. 46 Government.

Washington,D.C.Oct 2'05

Custodian New Mint,
Denver,Colo.

No objection to construction of partition in adjusting room building your custody to create room for refinery melting expense to be borne by mint bureau, acceptance of modified adjusting room floor will follow in few days.

J.K.Taylor ,
Supervising Architect.

411p

DENVER, NEW MINT

Q

IN REPLYING, QUOTE UPPER INITIAL, RIGHT HAND CORNER

TREASURY DEPARTMENT

OFFICE OF THE SECRETARY

WASHINGTON, Oct. 5, 1905.

The Custodian,
U. S. Mint (New),
Denver, Colorado.

Sir:

In view of the statements and recommendation contained in your letter of the 7th ultimo, the Departmental approval, and the public exigency which requires the immediate performance of the work, you are hereby authorized to accept the proposal of Mr. J. F. Wren, the lower of two received, in amount three hundred and twenty-five dollars ($325.00), for the supply in place complete of a new maple floor in the Adjusting Room in the building in your custody, with the understanding that 3/8" thick material is to be used in the work, and the entire floor completed in a satisfactory manner, as provided for in the specification upon which the proposal was based, except, that said specification is modified to provide for the laying of the floor only in that portion of the Adjusting Room not partitioned off for the new Refinery Melting Room, and further, that the work is to be completed within thirty days from the 10th instant, as provided for in the original proposal of the bidder.

In this connection, you are advised that the proposals submitted with your letter of August 29th, last, for laying the floor over the entire room, are hereby rejected; but, the certified check which accompanied Mr. Wren's original proposal, in the sum of $40.00, will be held to guarantee the satisfactory completion of the work embodied in this acceptance; the certified checks of the other bidders, however, will be returned to them in a separate communication.

Upon satisfactory completion of the work in accordance with this acceptance, please inform the Supervising Architect to that effect, and forward a voucher, in duplicate, duly certified and receipted, in accordance with this acceptance, for payment from the appropriation for "Repairs and Preservation of Public Buildings, 1906."

Respectfully,

H. A. Taylor

Acting Secretary.

L

Usch

JFS

[illegible]

[illegible] to advise Mr. [illegible] Kelley of the [illegible]

[illegible] under date of October [illegible], [illegible]

[illegible]

[illegible] giving, in amount thirty [illegible]

[illegible] tape [illegible] in the well [illegible] of the

[illegible], in accordance with the terms [illegible]

[illegible] your satisfaction, a [illegible]

[illegible] performance of the work, and [illegible]

[illegible] and issue vouchers therefor, after

[illegible] to your entire satisfaction, [illegible]

forward same to this Department for payment

[illegible] appropriation [illegible]

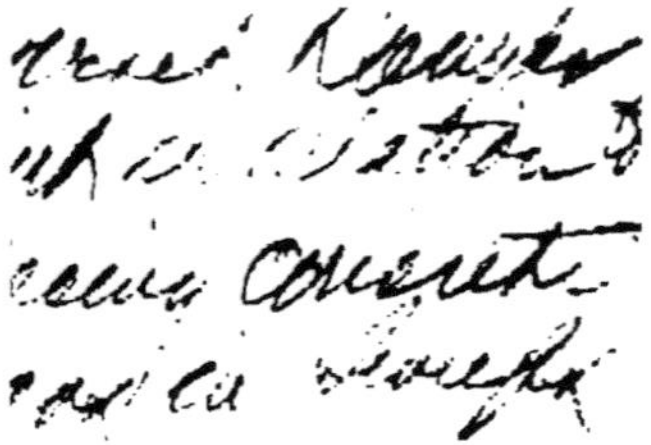

[illegible] M[illegible]

[illegible] [illegible] [illegible]

[illegible]

[illegible]

[illegible] M[illegible] B[illegible],

[illegible]

[illegible]

[illegible] Mineral Landing [illegible]

[illegible] the W[illegible] [illegible] of the [illegible]

[illegible]

[illegible] satisfactory [illegible] properly [illegible] made [illegible] as Superintendent [illegible] payable to the [illegible] of the Treasurer of the United States, [illegible] official checks, and that the same are always payable to the Treasurer of the United States as such.

Please return [illegible]

Respectfully,

[illegible]

[illegible] Superintendent [illegible]

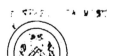

voucher in payment therefor in accordance with this acceptance, and transmit the same to this Department, duly receipted in the usual manner, for payment from the appropriation for "Repairs and Preservation of Public Buildings, 1906."

Please accompany the voucher by a letter indicating that the work is in accordance with the terms of the agreement, and to your satisfaction, and notify the successful bidders of the tenor of this letter, securing from them a statement as to the time within which they will complete the work, which statement is to be transmitted by you to the Supervising Architect for record and file.

Respectfully,

Acting Secretary.

THE COLORADO ROOFING AND PAVING COMPANY,

Denver, Colo.,November 14,1905.

The Custodian,

U.S.Mint, City.

Dear Sir:-

In reference to laying the cement floor in the Mint Building as per our bid of October 30th, we wish to say that we will commence the work within twenty-four hours after we are notified by you that the same is ready,and will complete the same within ten days .

Very truly yours,

The Colorado Roofing & Paving Co.

By G.W.Githens.

Copy.

Denver, Colo., November 14th, 1905.

Frank M. Downer, Custodian,

United States Mint, Denver, Colo.

Dear Sir:-

We propose to attach a three movement time lock to the Burglar Proof Vault in the Weigh Clerk's room at the Denver Mint similar to the time lock furnished on the other five vaults, of the Diebold Safe & Lock Co. make, for the sum of $250.00

Also to attach an alarm gong similar to those on different day gates in the several vaults, for the sum of $15.00, all to be fully guaranteed to be in perfect working order when completed.

Respectfully Submitted:

Diebold Safe & Lock Co.,

By Philip Garretson,

General Western Agent.

1st. endorsement: Respectfully recommend acceptance of both propositions as being necessary and reasonable.

Denver, Colo., 11/15105. (Signed) J.P.Bergin,

---

2nd endorsement.

Denver, Colo., 11/16/05

Respectfully referred to the Supervising Architect with the recommendation that the within proposals be accepted.

Frank M. Downer,
Custodian.

DEN M., NEW MAN.

TREASURY DEPARTMENT

Washington, October

Custodian,
U. S. Mint (New),
Denver, Colorado.

Sir:

By and with approval of the Department, under
17th instant, and, in view of the statement [illegible]
letter of the 4th instant, and the [illegible]
which requires the immediate delivery of the article [illegible]
of the work, you are hereby authorized to incur [illegible]
seventy-six dollars ($76.00), as per the proposal [illegible]
Iron Works Company, for raising iron doors of basement
at the building in your custody.

Upon satisfactory supply of the material and
the work, forward voucher therefor, duly certified
in the usual manner, - quoting thereon the date of
letter as above as the date of acceptance of proposal
same from the appropriation for "Repairs and Preser

DENVER MINT

OFFICE OF SUPERVISING ARCHITECT

IN REPLYING QUOTE UPPER INITIAL, RIGHT HAND CORNER.

Inclosure 7105.

TREASURY DEPARTMENT

WASHINGTON November 18, 1905.

Custodian,

U. S. Mint (New),

Denver, Colo.

Sir:

Referring to your communication of the 21st ultimo, there is inclosed herewith a copy of a letter of this date to the Diebold Safe & Lock Co., accepting their proposal in the sum of $295.00 for a steel storage case for the refinery in the building in your custody.

If delivery is not made within the time indicated, please advise this office to that effect. When the case is delivered make a careful examination of the same and report whether in your judgment it is in accordance with the agreement, and if it is, issue a voucher for the expense and forward it here for payment from the appropriation for "Vaults, Safes & Locks for Public Buildings, 1906."

Respectfully,

J K Taylor

Supervising Architect.

DENVER MINT

# TREASURY DEPARTMENT

OFFICE OF THE SECRETARY

WASHINGTON November 18,1905.

The Diebold Safe & Lock Co.,
Canton, Ohio.

Gentlemen:

In accordance with the approval of the Department, your proposal of the 20th ultimo was accepted by wire on the 17th instant in the sum of $295.00 to furnish a steel storage case and deliver the same in the refinery on the second floor of the U. S. Mint at Denver, Colo., as provided for by the specification; said bid being the lower of two received and the public exigency requiring the immediate delivery of the article. Said telegram is confirmed.

The inside dimensions of the case are to be 84" high, 72" wide and 72" deep in the clear. Approximate weight 3500 lbs. Time for delivery 40 days from date of receipt of order at the factory, and this time is to operate from the 17th instant.

It is desired that you will forward to the office of the Supervising Architect of this Department at the earliest practicable date shop drawings in triplicate of this case. Also state the make and number of combination lock to be used.

A copy of this letter will be forwarded to the Custodian of the building named with instructions, upon satisfactory delivery of the case, to issue a voucher for the expense, payment of which will be made from the appropriation for "Vaults, Safes & Locks for Public Buildings, 1906."

---

The proposal above referred to was submitted by your Agent at Denver to the Custodian of the Mint building, and formed the subject of your communication of the 13th instant.

Respectfully,

(Signed) H. A. Taylor.

Assistant Secretary.

T

Denver, Colo., Oct. 20th.1905

Frank M. Downer, Superintendent,

U.S. Mint Building,

Denver, Colo.

Dear Sir:-

In accordance with your request we have prepared estimate on steel storage case and door, to be delivered and erected in the United States Mint Building, Denver, Colorado, in the Refinery on the Second floor, and herewith submit the following proposition;

One steel case with door.

Inside measure of case, 7 feet high, 6 feet wide x 6 feet deep.

Case lining constructed of Bessemer steel plate 1/4" thick secured at all corners with 2 x 2 x 1/4" Bessemer steel angles. Joints of plates covered and secured by 3 x 1/4" Bessemer steel battens. This work to be put together with countersunk rivets, flush inside and outside.

This case lining to be provided with door 36" wide x 78" high, in the clear, constructed of 1/4" Bessemer steel with angle iron bolt

Denver, Colo., Oct. 20th, 1905

Frank M. Downer, Superintendent,

U.S. Mint Building,

Denver, Colo.

Dear Sir:-

In accordance with your request we have prepared estimate on steel storage case and door, to be delivered and erected in the United States Mint Building, Denver, Colorado, in the Refinery on the Second floor, and herewith submit the following proposition;

One steel case with door.

Inside measure of case, 7 feet high, 6 feet wide x 6 feet deep.

Case lining constructed of Bessemer steel plate 1/4" thick secured at all corners with 2 x 2 x 1/4" Bessemer steel angles. Joints of plates covered and secured by 3 x 1/4" Bessemer steel battens. This work to be put together with countersunk rivets, flush inside and outside.

This case lining to be provided with door 36" wide x 78" high, in the clear, constructed of 1/4" Bessemer steel with angle iron bolt frame, four horizontal bolts and one up and one down bolt, checked with a non-pickable, four tumbler, combination lock.

The floor on the inside of the case is to be flush with the top of the door sill and a suitable triangle shape fillet piece is to be furnished for a runway in order that trucks may be pulled into the case in a satisfactory manner.

The entire case inside and outside to be painted one coat of filler and one coat finishing color. The finish and complete design to be satisfactory to the Superintendent of the U.S. Mint at Denver.

Approximate weight 3600 lbs.

Price delivered and set in place $ 295.00

Time of delivery, forty days from receipt of order at the Factory.

Respectfully submitted,

Diebold Safe & Lock Co.,

Philip Garretson

General Western Agent.

Roger Roehl.

Proposal To
install Steel
Storage Box
for Refinery.
$295.00

The Custodian,

Mint Building (New),

Denver, Colorado.

Sir:

The Secretary of the Treasury, on the [illegible] instant, having waived the provision in contract dated December 6, 1904, with the Diebold Safe and Lock Company, stipulating the per diem amount of liquidated damages for delay in completion of steel vestibule, etc., for vault in Deposit Weigh Clerk's room in the building in your custody, you are hereby directed to prepare, certify and issue a voucher in favor of the company for $2,179.88, the full amount of the contract and proposal accepted in addition thereto. The voucher, after it has been receipted by the contractors, should be forwarded to the Department for payment, charged against the appropriation for "Mint Building, Denver, Colorado."

The following is a statement of the account and should be quoted literally upon the face of the voucher:

| | | |
|---|---|---|
| Contract dated Dec. 6, 1904. | For steel vestibule, etc., | $2,[illegible] |
| Proposal accepted March 30, 1905, | ........................................ | [illegible] |
| Amount due, | ........................................ | $2,179.88 |

Respectfully,

[signature]

Chief Executive Officer.

4

3.

DENVER, COLO., MINT BLDG.

REPLYING, QUOTE UPPER INITIAL, RIGHT HAND CORNER.

FORWARDING.

TREASURY DEPARTMENT

WASHINGTON December 8, 1905.

The Custodian,

U. S. Mint,

Denver, Colorado.

Sir:

There has this day been forwarded a set of plans showing the assignment of space for the building in your custody, with the request that you indicate thereon any variations which have occurred therein since occupation, and upon the receipt of the plans as amended, a corrected set of prints will be prepared and forwarded for the files of your office.

Respectfully,

M.

Supervising Architect.

DENVER. NEW MINT.

OFFICE OF SUPERVISING ARCHITECT

IN REPLYING QUOTE UPPER INITIAL. RIGHT HAND CORNER.

Forwarding.

TREASURY DEPARTMENT

WASHINGTON December 19,1905.

Custodian,

U. S. Mint (New),

Denver, Colorado.

Sir:

There are forwarded to you this day under separate cover twelve (12) copies of specification, together with four (4) prints of drawing No.R-292-A, for alterations and repairs in the Dry Sweeps Room at the building in your custody, prepared from report dated the 17th ultimo made by the representative of this office who visited the building, and you are authorized to invite by circular letter competitive proposals for the performance of the work.

Fix a date for opening proposals, open all received in the presence of bidders who may be in attendance, schedule the same and forward them here with your recommendations. All certified checks deposited with bids must be forwarded also. The checks must be scheduled, and if bids are not accompanied by checks, due mention must be made of that fact. Strict compliance with this instruction is required, so that proper record of checks may be made.

Respectfully,

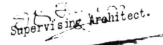

Supervising Architect.

[illegible],

Mint Building.

Denver, Colo.

Sir:

[illegible] have to acknowledge the receipt of your letter of the [illegible] instant, enclosing voucher in favor of C. J. Reilly, in amount $[illegible] for installing heating coil in the building in your custody. You are advised that payment of the voucher in question will probably be delayed for a short time as the available balance of the appropriation for said building, through [illegible] inadvertence, will not permit of the adjustment of the voucher at once [illegible] a deficiency appropriation has been submitted to Congress, with the approval of the Secretary, and it is thought that a check in payment of the voucher will be forwarded to you before very long.

Respectfully,

[illegible signature]

Acting Chief Executive Officer

DENVER, NEW MINT

Q

OFFICE OF SUPERVISING ARCHITECT

IN REPLYING, QUOTE UPPER INITIAL, RIGHT HAND CORNER

FORWARDING.

10105

TREASURY DEPARTMENT

WASHINGTON, Jan. 3, 1906.

S

The Custodian,

U. S. Mint (New),

Denver, Colorado.

Sir:

There has been transmitted to you, under separate cover, a new set of assignment plans for the building in your custody, which are to take the place of those now in your possession; the new plans showing the changes recently made in rooms under authority from the Department.

Respectfully,

Supervising Architect.

DENVER NEW MINT

K

OFFICE OF SUPERVISING ARCHITECT

IN REPLYING QUOTE UPPER INITIAL, RIGHT HAND CORNER.

Inclosure 7128.

TREASURY DEPARTMENT

WASHINGTON December 7,1905.

Custodian,

U. S. Mint,

Denver, Colo.

Sir:

In connection with letter addressed to you on the 21st ultimo please find inclosed herewith a copy of a communication of the 25th ultimo to the Diebold Safe & Lock Co., approving a supplementary drawing submitted by them of the storage case ordered for the building in your custody. There is also inclosed a copy of the drawing. On the 27th ultimo the Company stated that they had changed their shop drawings making the depth specified to be clear of the bolt work. They also stated that their No. 4 Iron Case "Eagle" combination lock, with straight spindle, is to be used.

Respectfully,

Supervising Architect.

OFFICE OF SUPERVISING ARCHITECT

IN REPLYING, QUOTE UPPER INITIAL, RIGHT HAND CORNER.

# TREASURY DEPARTMENT

WASHINGTON

November 25, 1905.

The Diebold Safe & Lock Co.,

Canton, Ohio.

Gentlemen:

Your communication of the 22d instant is received in relation to the storage case ordered from you for the Mint at Denver, Colo., and I thank you for calling attention to the discrepancy in regard to measurements. It is noted, however, that the specification and letter of acceptance indicate that the dimensions are to be clear inside. The word <u>clear</u> means that the depth is to be clear of the bolt work, instead of between the body plates as shown on the supplementary print submitted. With this modification, the [illegible]ing will be satisfactory.

Your attention is called to the fact that you have failed to [illegible]e this office of the name and number of combination lock to be used on the case, as requested in Department letter of the 16th instant.

Respectfully,

(Signed) J. K. Taylor

Supervising Architect.

DENVER NEW MINT

M

OFFICE OF SUPERVISING ARCHITECT

IN REPLYING, QUOTE UPPER INITIAL, RIGHT HAND CORNER

Inclosure 7111.

TREASURY DEPARTMENT

WASHINGTON November 21,1905.

Custodian,

U. S. Mint,

Denver, Colo.

Sir:

In connection with letter addressed to you on the 18th instant in relation to this matter, please find inclosed copy of a letter of this date to the Diebold Safe & Lock Co., at Canton, Ohio, regarding the drawing submitted for the storage case ordered for the building in your custody. A copy of the drawing is also inclosed herewith.

Respectfully,

Supervising Architect.

OFFICE OF SUPERVISING ARCHITECT

IN REPLYING, QUOTE UPPER INITIAL, RIGHT HAND CORNER.

# TREASURY DEPARTMENT

WASHINGTON November 21, 1905.

The Diebold Safe & Lock Co.,

Canton, Ohio.

Gentlemen:

The receipt is acknowledged of your communication of the 18th instant submitting prints of the steel storage case ordered from you for the Mint building at Denver, Colo.

Drawing No. 7435 illustrates the work as it is specified, except that the angles and battens are not believed to be of sufficient size to give the necessary stiffness. These angles should be at least 3" x 3" x 1/4" and the battens should have a width of at least 6".

Respectfully,

(Signed) J. K. Taylor.

Supervising Architect.

DENVER MINT.

OFFICE OF SUPERVISING ARCHITECT

IN REPLYING, QUOTE UPPER INITIAL, RIGHT HAND CORNER.

# TREASURY DEPARTMENT

WASHINGTON January 18,1906.

The Custodian,

U.S. Mint Building,

Denver,Colorado.

Sir:

Replying to your letter of the 9th instant,requesting duplicate prints of drawings Nos.1 to 37,inclusive, for the superstructure and terra cotta partitions of the building in your custody,you are advised that no prints of said drawings are available,and the original tracings are in such condition that reproductions cannot be made therefrom. It is regretted that your request cannot be complied with.

Respectfully,

Supervising Architect.

B.

DENVER. NEW MINT

Q

OFFICE OF SUPERVISING ARCHITECT

IN REPLY DO QUOTE UPPER INITIAL RIGHT HAND CORNER

# TREASURY DEPARTMENT

WASHINGTON, Jan. 19, 1906.

The Custodian,

U. S. Mint (New),

Denver, Colorado.

Sir:

Referring to your communication of the 15th instant, transmitting proposals for alterations in the sweeps room at the building in your custody, you are advised that Mr. J. C. Plant, Chief Computer of this Office, will be in your city in the near future, and will make the matter the subject of an examination and report.

Action upon the bids and upon the recommendation contained in your letter will be withheld, therefore, pending the receipt of this report.

Respectfully,

L

Supervising Architect.

DENVER NEW MINT

OFFICE OF SUPERVISING ARCHITECT

IN REPLYING, QUOTE UPPER INITIAL, RIGHT HAND CORNER.

Inclosure 7062.

TREASURY DEPARTMENT

S

WASHINGTON February 12,1906.

Custodian,

U. S. Mint,

Denver, Colo.

Sir:

Your communication of the 6th instant has been received at this office by reference from the Director of the Mint, in which you request a fire proof safe for the office of the Melter and Refiner in the building in your custody.

It is not the practice of this office to furnish the so-called light wall fire proof safe. The least thickness that will be permitted in a safe of this character is a 6" wall, and such protection as this would seem not to be necessary in a building of fire-proof construction.

A shell safe as described in the inclosed specification it is believed will furnish ample fire protection for use in a building such as that in your custody, and the specification is submitted to you for your approval or any comments. Please return the inclosure with your reply, and state also the floor and number of room in which the safe is to be delivered.

Respectfully,

DENVER, NEW MINT

Q

TREASURY DEPARTMENT

WASHINGTON, Feb. 14, 1906.

IN REPLYING QUOTE UPPER INITIAL, RIGHT HAND CORNER.

Inclosure 6663

The Custodian,
U. S. Mint (New),
Denver, Colorado.

Sir:

Referring to your communication of the 15th ultimo, forwarding bids for alterations in the sweeps cellar at the building in your custody, you are advised that the Office is in receipt of a report of the 13th instant from Mr. J. C. Plant, Chief Computer, which suggests certain other work in lieu of the alterations, and in view of this the bids which accompanied your letter are to be rejected by you.

The certified checks which accompanied the bids are herewith transmitted, to be returned by you to the bidders, viz.: The Hinchman-Renton Fireproofing Company, in the sum of $110.00; Stocker & Frasser, in the sum of $114.50; The Morrison Contracting and Manufacturing Company, in the sum of $170.00; and The Flint-Lomax Electric and Manufacturing Company, in amount $231.50.

The report of Mr. Plant, above indicated, will receive consideration, the result of which you will be further advised.

Respectfully,

Supervising Architect.

CIRCULARS TO CUSTODIANS.

OFFICE OF SUPERVISING ARCHITECT

IN REPLYING QUOTE UPPER INITIAL RIGHT HAND CORNER.

TREASURY DEPARTMENT

WASHINGTON

S

February 14, 1906.

Custodian,

U. S. Branch Mint
Denver, Col.

Sir:

Please report immediately whether there are public telephone pay stations in the building in your custody. If so, how many, where they are located, and by what authority they are permitted in the building.

Respectfully,

J K Taylor
Supervising Architect.

L
1.SEK.

1909.
Department Circular No. 47.
Division of Printing and Stationery.

TREASURY DEPARTMENT,
OFFICE OF THE SECRETARY,
*Washington, September 18, 1909.*

*To officers and employees of the Treasury Department and others concerned:*

The United States Government steel-pen contract for the current fiscal year having been awarded to the Miller Bros. Cutlery Co., of Meriden, Conn., on what are known to the trade as the "Miller Bros." pens, these pens will be used during the year in the entire Treasury service to the exclusion of other makes. The list of Miller Bros. pens embraces points corresponding closely with those of other leading makes now used throughout the service. In order, therefore, that officers of the service, when ordering pens, may be enabled to properly designate on requisitions the kinds of points desired, the following table is published for their information:

CORRESPONDING POINTS.

| Miller Bros. | Esterbrook. | Hunt. | Eagle. | Gillott. | Spencerian. |
|---|---|---|---|---|---|
| 04 ........ corresponding to.. | 312 | 75 | 110 | 1071 | ........ |
| 030 ........ do ..... | 130 | 47 | ........ | ........ | 2 |
| 084 ........ do ..... | 048 | 97 | ........ | ........ | ........ |
| 1 ........ do ..... | 14 | 57 | 40 | 1044 | ........ |
| 4 ........ do ..... | 313 | 38 | 110 | 1043 | 28 |
| 15TP ........ do ..... | 477 | ........ | ........ | 1032 | ........ |
| 19 ........ do ..... | 2 | 96 | ........ | 908 | ........ |
| 20 ........ do ..... | 656 | 42 | ........ | 1070 | ........ |
| 23 ........ do ..... | 239 | 62 | ........ | 1008 | ........ |
| 28 ........ do ..... | 126 | 21 | ........ | 604 | 1 |
| 74 ........ do ..... | 442 | 65 | ........ | 1083 | ........ |
| 80 ........ do ..... | 182 | 95 | ........ | ........ | ........ |
| 87 ........ do ..... | 048 | 97 | ........ | 878 | 40 |
| 101 ........ do ..... | 135 | 54 | 450 | ........ | ........ |
| 103 ........ do ..... | 314 | ........ | ........ | ........ | ........ |
| 333 ........ do ..... | 333 | 55 | ........ | 303 | ........ |
| 444 ........ do ..... | 444 | 56 | ........ | 404 | ........ |

JAMES B. REYNOLDS,
*Acting Secretary.*